ENGLISH LANGUAGE SERIES

English in Advertising

ENGLISH LANGUAGE SERIES
General Editor : Randolph Quirk

THE MOVEMENT OF ENGLISH PROSE
Ian A. Gordon

ENGLISH IN ADVERTISING—*A Linguistic
Study of Advertising in Great Britain*
Geoffrey N. Leech

THE ENGLISH LANGUAGE IN AUSTRALIA
AND NEW ZEALAND
G. W. Turner

English in Advertising

A Linguistic Study of Advertising in Great Britain

GEOFFREY N. LEECH

Lecturer in English : University College London

LONGMANS

LONGMANS, GREEN AND CO LTD
48 Grosvenor Street, London W.1
Associated companies, branches and representatives
throughout the world

Made and printed in Great Britain by
William Clowes and Sons, Limited
London and Beccles

To My Wife

Foreword

The English of advertising has aroused – though hardly engaged – the interest of linguists for many years, and most books on the English language make some general statements about it. Few linguists, however, have approached the task of making such statements with a solid body of research experience in the field of the kind or quality acquired by Mr Leech, who for some years made the language of commercial persuasion – especially in television – the object of detailed and specialised study. He brings to his present task also, as is essential, a deep knowledge of current linguistic theory, especially with reference to its bearing on the study of style, and he uses the insights so provided to make illuminating statements on the characteristic features of advertising language.

The late Joshua Whatmough comprehended poetry and sales-talk in a single 'dynamic' vision. 'The most recent English and American poetry partakes of the great changes taking place in the English language, which are part and parcel of the contemporary environment; the same is true of political propaganda, or of advertising copy. The same "emotive" and "dynamic" components pervade all three of them' (*Language*, London 1956, p. 107). But so far as advertising is concerned, at any rate, it is the 'emotive' component that has attracted most attention, whether the resulting attitude to the mass media which are its vehicle is one of mild approval (where an author uses the title *The Miracle of Shared Living*) or one of strident alarm (*The Tyranny of Words*).

As he makes clear below, Mr Leech's book by no means includes among its aims any attempt to evaluate forms of advertisement from the viewpoint either of successful salesmanship or of social welfare. These are matters for the psychologist and others. Rather, in examining in some detail a form of English that has developed special characteristics for the specialised needs of advertising, the present book makes an important contribution to the study of linguistic aspects of style, not only valuable for those who wish to study the English of advertising but interestingly applicable to other types of English whose form is in some respects directly motivated by the uses to which they are applied.

This book has therefore an obvious and welcome place in the series in which it appears. As English has increasingly come into world-wide use, there has arisen an acute need for more information on the language and the ways in which it is used. The English Language Series seeks to meet this need and to play a part in further stimulating the study and teaching of English by providing up-to-date and scholarly treatments of topics most relevant to present-day English – including its history and traditions, its sound patterns, its grammar, its lexicology, its rich and functionally orientated variety in speech and writing, and its standards in Britain, the U S A, and the other principal areas where the language is used.

RANDOLPH QUIRK

University College London
December, 1965

Preface

This book is not intended exclusively, or even primarily, for people who already have a grounding in linguistics. As an exercise in linguistic description, it obviously cannot entirely do without technical linguistic vocabulary; and some words and phrases have necessarily been adopted as additional technical terms for the specific purpose of this analysis. However, the linguistic apparatus is simple, and is explained, for those who feel the need of explanations, in Chapter 2. The index, with special references to technical terms, gives additional help.

I am very grateful to George Berman for help in proof-reading ; to R. G. Fowler for his careful reading and criticism of this book in type-script; to M. A. K. Halliday, for comments on Chapter 2; and to John W. Thompson for suggesting improvements to Chapter 3. I owe a general debt of thanks to my colleagues at University College London, especially to Randolph Quirk for guidance and encouragement during the writing of this book.

GNL

University College London
December, 1965

Contents

Acknowledgments

We are grateful to the following for permission to reproduce extracts from advertising copy:

Air France; The Anglo American Drug Co; Elizabeth Arden Ltd; Aristoc Ltd; Bass, Mitchells & Butlers Ltd; B.B.C. Refreshments Ltd; Beecham Tioletry Division; Beecham Group Ltd; Mr. L. Benjamin; J. W. Benson Ltd; Berkertex Sales Ltd; J. E. Bird Automobiles Ltd; Bowater-Scott Corporation Ltd; The British Motor Corporation Ltd; Britvic Ltd; Brown & Polson Ltd; T. B. Browne Ltd on behalf of the Proprietors of 'Toff-o-Luxe'; James Buchanan & Co. Ltd; Burco Ltd; Cadbury Brothers Ltd; Carreras Sales Ltd; The Cement Marketing Co. Ltd; Cerebos Foods Ltd; Chiswick Products Ltd; Chivers Hartley Ltd; Churchman, Branch of The Imperial Tobacco Company (of Great Britain and Ireland) Ltd; Cogent Advertising Service Ltd on behalf of Coventry Climax Engines Ltd; W. H. Collins & Co. Ltd; Colman Prentis & Varley Ltd on behalf of Watney Mann Ltd and the Proprietors of 'Handy Andy' and 'Knorr Soup'; Crawfords International Advertising on behalf of D.E.R. Television Rentals, The Milk Marketing Board, Jackson the Tailor, and the Proprietors of the *Sunday Dispatch* and 'Jordan Toothbrush'; Crouch End Motor & Engineering Co. Ltd; Dae Health Laboratories Ltd; the Proprietors of the *Daily Sketch* and *Daily Graphic*; Domestos Ltd; Erwin Wasy Ltd on behalf of the Proprietors of 'Carnation', 'Eskimo Fishsteaks', 'I.C.I. Plus', 'Johnson's Glo-Coat', 'Quaker Puffed Wheat', 'Snowbowl', 'Sugar Puffs', and 'Trebor'; Everetts Advertising Ltd on behalf of the Proprietors of 'C.C.F. Fertilisers', 'Dabitoff', 'Kensitas', and 'Lucky Charm'; Film Exchange Ltd; Finbow & Sons Ltd; Formica Ltd; Gallaher Ltd; Garland-Compton Ltd on behalf of the Proprietors of 'Rowntree's Fruit Pastilles', Gilbey Twiss Ltd; Goldwell Ltd; Grant Advertising Ltd on behalf of the Proprietors of 'KVP Food-Saver Wax Paper'; Green Brothers (Swansea) Ltd; Arthur Guinness Son & Co. (Park Royal) Ltd; John Haig & Co. Ltd; Halex (British Xylonite Co. Ltd); Harveys of Bristol Ltd; the Controller of Her Majesty's Stationery Office; Innoxa (England) Ltd; Interflora; International Chemical Co. Ltd; International Nickel Ltd; Izal Ltd; Judy, Children's Wear; Kyabram Preserving Co. Ltd; Lever Brothers Ltd; The London Assurance; The London Press Exchange Ltd; Lotus Cars Ltd; Masius, Wynne-Williams Ltd on behalf of the Proprietors of 'Capstan Cigarettes'; Mather & Crowther Ltd; McCann-Erickson Advertising Ltd on behalf of Charrington United Breweries, Californian Packing Co. Inc., Nabisco Foods Ltd and Nicholas Products Ltd; McDougalls Ltd;

Ministry of Defence (Army); Ministry of Defence (Air); MISR Foreign Trade Co. S.A.E.; C. Mitchell & Co. Ltd; Mönlycke Textiles Ltd; Wm. Moorhouse & Sons Ltd; Morphy Richards (Astral) Ltd; New Society; Joseph Newsome & Sons Ltd; Notley Advertising Ltd on behalf of the Proprietors of 'Bri-nylon', 'Clarks Sandals', 'Focus' and 'VP Wines'; The Observer Ltd; The Outspan Organisation; Parkinson Cowan Appliances Ltd; James Pascall, Confectioners; R. Paterson & Sons, Ltd; Peerless (Dovetail) Built-In Furniture Ltd; Petfoods Ltd; Electrical Division of Radiation Ltd; Polycell Products Ltd; The Rank Organisation, Bush Radio Division; Remington Electric Shaver Ltd; Ronson Products Ltd; G. S. Royds Ltd on behalf of the Proprietors of 'Beecham's Powders', 'Amami', 'Electrolux', 'Guards Cigarettes' and 'Mum Rollette'; The Ryvita Co. Ltd; Schweppes (Home) Ltd; Service Advertising Co. Ltd on behalf of the Proprietors of 'Condor Sliced', 'Gallaher's Blues', 'Lurpak Butter', 'Manikin Cigars', 'Morley Socks', 'Morley Sweaters', 'Nelson Cigarettes', 'Old Holborn Tobacco', 'Olivier', 'Park Drive', 'Park Drive Tipped', and 'Suncrush'; Shell-Mex and B.P. Ltd; Spottiswoode Advertising Ltd on behalf of the Proprietors of 'Brooke Bond Tea'; Steiner Products Ltd; Tanqueray, Gordon & Co. Ltd; Taylor Advertising (Provinces) Ltd on behalf of Schofield Brothers Ltd ('Slik Fits'); The J. Walter Thompson Company Limited on behalf of the Proprietors of 'Addis Brushes', 'Andrex', 'Bachelor Cigarettes', 'Brillo Soap Pads', 'Campbells Soups', 'Cheese Bureau', 'Clean Lawn', 'Clean Leaf', 'Crackerbarrel', 'Cyril Lord Carpets', 'English Electric Slimline', 'Eno', 'Findus Fish Sticks', 'Fray Bentos', 'Horlicks', 'Hornby Trains', 'Liberator Washing Machines', 'Kelloggs Coco Pops', 'Kelloggs Corn Flakes', 'Kelloggs Frosties', 'Kelloggs Rice Krispies', 'Kelloggs Ricicles', 'Kelloggs Sugar Smacks', 'Kelloggs Whole Wheat Flakes', 'Kit Kat', 'Kraft Superfine Margarine', 'Lux Flakes', 'Lux Soap', 'Metercal', 'Nimble Bread', 'Nux', 'Oxo', 'Polo Mint', 'Smarties', 'Thrive', 'Vick Vapour Rub', 'Windolene', and 'Wisdom Toothbrushes'; The Times Publishing Co. Ltd.; The Toni Company; Triumph Engineering Company; Universal Laboratories Ltd: Brand of Dihydroxy Aluminium Sodiam Carbonate and Calcium Carbonate, Proprietors of 'Daxaids'; Van Den Berghs Ltd; The Wall Paper Manufacturers Ltd; Eustace Watkins Ltd; The Wellcome Foundation Ltd, Proprietors of 'Marzine'; Whiteways Cyder Co. Ltd; Odhams Press Ltd, Proprietors of *Woman* and *Woman's Realm*, and Young & Rubican Ltd on behalf of the Proprietors of 'Clinic Shampoo', 'Disprin', 'Erasmic', 'Gaymel Paint', 'Gibbs S.R. Toothpaste', 'Maxwell House Coffee', 'Olympic Tipped', and 'Swift Carpet Shampoo'.

Acknowledgment is due to the Proprietors of the *Hornsey Journal* and to Warner-Pathé Film Distributors Ltd for illustrations of advertising copy. The playbill of 1815 is reproduced by courtesy of The Lambs, New York.

Introduction

Chapter 1

General

Who wants to know about advertising language? A sociologist might be interested in its effect on the behaviour and values of society; a psychologist might be interested in its effect on individual motivations; an advertising practitioner might simply want to find clues to more successful advertising. And there are many other possible approaches, reflecting different academic and professional concerns with the subject.

This book is written in a spirit of neutral enquiry, with the purely linguistic object of describing what British advertising language is *like*. This is a limited aim, which may seem to exclude many interesting lines of investigation and discussion. But it has the merit of precision, and forms a platform of enquiry which may well be said to presuppose any discussion of the subject from sociological or other points of view, and even to provide a factual source for them. I shall be interested also in relating advertising language to its setting and function, so my conception of what advertising language is like will be broad enough to include, in a sense, how it *works*.

Linguistics is the discipline which aims to describe language and to discover the principles of its structure. In spite of rapid developments in this field over the past thirty years, it has so far been the least influential of the major social sciences, in that its methods and discoveries have had comparatively little effect on popular modes of thought. Yet the study of language can be regarded as central to man's study of himself, whether as an individual or as a social being. As problems of communication grow ever more complex, liguistics may well begin to play a larger role in our appraisal of ourselves and the society in which we live. It is certainly desirable that we should cultivate an objective and critical awareness of the linguistic transactions into which we enter day by day, either as initiators or passive recipients. In so far as it treats of a subject of practical importance in a linguistic way, the present study is a gesture in this direction.

One way to approach the study of advertising language is to think of the advertising copywriter as having at his disposal a huge repertoire of linguistic choices, namely 'the English language'. What choices he makes and how frequently he makes them, is the subject for study. But this view is misleadingly simple, because it implies that the copywriter has greater freedom of selection than he effectually enjoys. Many different factors predispose him to choose in one way, rather than in another: the medium for which his advertisement is destined; the type of audience for which it is intended; the very fact that he is writing an advertisement and not a political speech or some other kind of composition. Imagine a copywriter with an incomplete sentence in his mind 'Consult your . . .', and a choice of completing it with 'doctor', 'physician', or 'medical practitioner'. 'Imagine' is the operative word, because the situation is unreal. The choice between these three synonymous expressions is made for him by the fact that he is writing advertising copy, instead of (say) a pamphlet on the National Health Service. Put differently, this means that *doctor* belongs to the 'idiom' or 'usage' of advertising, whereas *physician* and *medical practitioner* do not. Or we could include it in the far more general statement that advertising vocabulary is colloquial, not formal.

Such predispositions obviously vary according to the type of advertising, and cannot be studied without a general picture of the relation between language and situation, and the relation between advertising English and other types of English. These will be the themes of Part I of this book.

Another question is the strength of these predispositions. It is easily accepted that the copywriter is 'steered' towards certain choices by the set of conditions for which he is writing. But it is patently false that he writes according to a predecided formula, which leaves no room for originality. One of the interesting aspects of advertising language is its delicate compromise between the opposed tendencies of conformity and unorthodoxy: between following a prescribed path of advertising clichés and exercising the freedom to deviate from it, and even, on occasion, to deviate from the rules of the English language itself.

In Part II, I give an account of what I call 'standard advertising English', which is a distillation of what is most typical or conventional in British advertising copy. Standard advertising English is a good example of language adapted to a well-defined social purpose, and one of the interests of studying it is that of finding out how its features reflect psychological strategy and other aspects of the situation for which it is designed. Some people (perhaps copywriters themselves) may be unhappy about the notion of a 'standard' or 'norm' in copywriting. The best assurance that it exists is that the ease with which we are able to take revenge upon it by mimicry and burlesque. Parody of advertising language, in which everybody over the age of six must have indulged at some time or other, is essentially a reproduction, and exaggeration, of its most characteristic features.

Part III provides a corrective to Part II, by investigating the element of novelty and unorthodoxy in advertising English. Also in this part there will be some consideration of matters peripheral to the descriptive aim of this book: a glance at the history of advertising language, and a discussion of poetic and rhetorical devices in advertising.

My main preparation for this book was four years of intermittent research on the language of television advertising in Britain.* I examined a sample of 617 advertisements first broadcast December 1960–May 1961, and quantitatively analysed their grammar and vocabulary. For part of this period, I had the benefit of co-operation with a colleague, Eugene Winter, who was working on rather different lines on the language of press advertising.† I have also complemented my original study of television commercials by a selective study of advertising copy in other media. All advertisements used as examples (except by way of providing historical background) have appeared in the past five years.

Such are my qualifications for writing this book, and it is fitting to consider in what way they entitle me to call myself an expert on advertising language, and what kind of expert knowledge is transmitted through these pages. To give a fair answer to this question, I shall have to distinguish between three types of linguistic attainment. The first, OPERATIONAL SKILL, is the property of anyone who has learnt to speak and understand his native tongue. The second, PRAGMATIC SKILL, is the ability to use one's language successfully in any particular sphere of endeavour. A good novelist, a good orator, a good copywriter, have each acquired such skill in their particular fields. Training and experience, combined with innate ability, are generally the prerequisites of excellence in these accomplishments. In many fields of pragmatic skill there is a considerable volume of literature devoted to the theory of successful performance: manuals of journalism, of public speaking, of copywriting, and so on. The third attainment, which is alone the concern of this book, is ANALYTIC KNOWLEDGE of language: the ability to 'explain' a language, by describing the rules of its structure and use. This is a very different kind of attainment from that of being able to *use* the rules correctly and with facility.

---

* Reported in a thesis for the degree of Master of Arts at the University of London, May 1963.
† Reported in another M.A. thesis, E. O. O. Winter, *The Language of Contemporary Newspaper Advertisements in English* (University of London, April 1964).

Many fluent, native speakers of English are able to say little about English grammar – which is to say that their knowledge of English grammar is operationally good and analytically poor. On the other hand, all of us who have been through grammar classes at school have at least some analytic knowledge of English. To increase this insight into the working of language and of languages is the goal of linguistics.

I have stressed the distinctness of analytic knowledge and pragmatic 'know-how' partly to show that the description of a piece of language has little to do with the judgement of its success or failure. The standards of success and failure in advertising, as elsewhere, are pragmatic, and depend mostly on the individual circumstances of each advertisement – its purpose, its timing, the marketing situation, etc. But in describing advertising language analytically, we are interested in generalisations which apply irrespective of these factors. Furthermore, the success of a particular piece of copy can only be judged in the context of the communicative complex (including, for example, pictorial material) of which it is a part. It is probably meaningless to talk of 'good advertising copy' in abstraction from the total communicative resources of the medium.

The distinction between analytic knowledge and operational knowledge helps to illuminate the role of statistics in this study. The fact that people are able to parody advertisements shows that they have some operational knowledge of advertising English: that they can speak the copywriter's 'lingo' when they feel like it (which is not to say that they have the pragmatic skill of writing good copy). Given the appropriate frame of mind and tools of description, this knowledge can be put to effect analytically. No exhaustive study of advertising material is required for a statement such as 'Imperatives are very frequent in advertising English'. Everyone who has been subjected to a normal amount of advertising knows this fact perfectly well, though he may not have given conscious thought to it, and may not be able to formulate it unless he is familiar with the analytic term 'imperative'. We can analyse our native language, or any familiar variety of it, up to a point, merely by submitting to conscious examination what we already know operationally. Part of my purpose here is to present not facts but the state of mind in which advertising English is regarded factually.

But it is equally clear that a detailed study of texts sharpens and extends analytic knowledge, and permits observations which could not be obtained by just casual generalisation on one's previous experience of advertising. Instead of saying, for example, that active clauses are far more frequent than passive clauses in television advertising, I can say that, according to the sample analysed, they are 22·1 times as frequent. The ultimate goal, in quantitative analysis, would be a comparative statistical study of advertising English and other varieties of English, so that it would be possible to plot relative frequencies against external controls. Such an ambitious programme is not needed for the degree of detail aimed at here; and in any case the returns yielded would decrease in proportion to the amount of effort expended. Quantitative and non-quantitative methods are complementary ways of finding out what a given body of language is like. The former may merely confirm what is intuitively obvious, or may confirm a guess, or may reveal some completely unsuspected property of the material under study. It cannot be considered more fundamental or 'scientific' than the evidence of operational experience, and indeed is valueless without the insight that tells the investigator what are the significant categories to count and contrast. It is this complementary role of the two types of evidence which explains my occasional, but by no means general, use of statistical backing for my statements about advertising language.

Chapter 2

Linguistic Framework

Underlying this study is a particular approach to the description of language,* which I shall seek to explain briefly in this introduction, keeping in view those things which will be important for the study of advertising language.

Levels

Language is a complex form of activity. To describe its principles of organisation, we have to distinguish between different LEVELS of patterning, requiring independent means of description, and associated with different branches of linguistic study. There is no need to distinguish terminologically between levels and their associated fields of study; for example, 'grammar' means both an aspect of language, and the pursuit of studying it.

GRAMMAR and VOCABULARY (or LEXIS) together make up the central level of linguistic FORM.

PHONOLOGY relates these abstract formal patterns of language to the physical noises and articulatory movements of speech.

Phonology is paralleled by ORTHOGRAPHY, which relates form to the physical manifestation of written language – marks on paper.

CONTEXT, in its widest sense, is the relation between linguistic form and everything which is not language, the 'world at large'. It is convenient to

---

* A work of this kind is no place for argument on basic linguistic issues or on the merits of alternative descriptions of the English language. I assume as a basis for my investigation an approach which is being used in a number of current investigations of English and other languages, and which had its first major theoretical exposition in Halliday (1961); I have drawn heavily on this article in the linguistic introduction, and also on further work on English grammar by Halliday and others, now (or shortly to be) more accessible in Halliday, McIntosh, and Strevens (1964), and in McIntosh and Halliday (1966). (*See Bibliography.*) At the same time, I have simplified and modified this approach in adapting it to the task in hand. The main points on which I deviate from treatments in the works mentioned are: (*a*) the meaning of 'context'; (*b*) the structure and classification of nominal groups in English; and (*c*) the descriptive application of the dependence relation.

distinguish between two ways in which this relation of language to the 'world' comes about.

First, linguistic form has cognitive or denotative meaning, by which it refers to entities and events in the world. SEMANTICS is the usual name for the study of this function of language.

Secondly, language operates in observable social settings, and the relation between linguistic patterns and situational patterns can be termed CONTEXT in a narrower sense. In this book I shall prefer this sense to the broader one just given. Advertising is one kind of linguistic situation, so this study is orientated towards context: its purpose can be summarised as that of finding out about other aspects of language when that of context is, within certain limits, held constant.

I shall not devote equal attention to all the levels named above, and in any case this is not desirable. Phonology and orthography are unimportant in a study of this kind, because they do not vary greatly according to different public roles of English. These levels enter into our ken in being the carriers of formal patterns, but rarely call for independent comment. It is true that some aspects of the physical manifestation of advertising language are very important: visual display, typography, vocal quality, and other features of lay-out and delivery which signal emphasis and feeling. These are generally considered to be outside language altogether, and will have only an incidental place in this book. Semantics will not receive the attention it deserves, being the least understood of the levels of language. So our main concern will be with the *form* of language, rather than with its meaning or transmission. This is not the limitation it appears to be, for there will be continual cross-reference from one level to another in the course of the description.

Four Basic Concepts

The four concepts of UNIT, STRUCTURE, CLASS, and SYSTEM provide a framework for describing the patterns of language. They will be illustrated here with examples from the grammar of English.

Unit

Linguistic activity is essentially capable of being cut up into units over which recurrent patterns can be observed. The units are classifiable by their relative extent or size, such that one can be said to consist of one or more of smaller size. On this basis, we set up a hierarchy of grammatical

RANK, on which five units are placed in order of decreasing extent: SENTENCE, CLAUSE, GROUP, WORD, and MORPHEME. Sentence, clause, and word are familiar grammatical terms; of the less familiar ones, the group is a unit intermediate between word and clause (not far from the common meaning of 'phrase') and morphemes are the grammatical segments into which words are divisible (stems and affixes). It is customary to split the study of grammar at word rank into SYNTAX (grammar outside the word) and MORPHOLOGY (grammar within the word). The notion of 'size' is not to be taken too literally: 'larger' must be interpreted to mean 'either of equal *or* of greater extent'. The sentence 'They took it'* consists of only one clause, and in this clause, *they, took,* and *it* are all groups consisting of a single word (whereas in 'Someone else has taken my place', the equivalent groups 'someone else', 'has taken', and 'my place' each consist of two words). In the cases where a unit consists of only one unit of lower rank, the two units are coextensive and, literally speaking, of the 'same size'.

Structure

Every unit (except the smallest, the morpheme) has a pattern or structure describable in terms of units of the next lowest rank. In the present scheme of analysis, the elements of clause structure in English are:

S: SUBJECT
P: PREDICATOR (traditionally 'verb', but this term is needed for a class of word)
C: COMPLEMENT ('object', 'complement' in traditional grammar)
A: ADJUNCT (the adverbial element)

Using the abbreviations S, P, C, and A, we can exemplify some of the different structures they make:

S	P	C	A		S	P	
He	tapped	me	on the knee		I	know	
P	C	C			P	S	C
Give	me	the phone			Are	you	ready?

Two sophistications of the scheme enter with the following examples:

A	S	P	Z	P	C
before	I	could stop	him	doing	it

---

* This example is invented, as are all others in this linguistic introduction.

| | S | P | ⟨A   ⟩ | A | P | A |
| By now | they | 're ⟨probably⟩ trying | desperately | to catch up | with us |

'z' in the first clause represents a nominal element which is indeterminate as to subject or complement status. It is a complement with respect to the predicator *stop*, and a subject with respect to the predicator *doing*. The angle brackets ⟨ ⟩ in the second example enclose an element which interrupts another element: the predicator *'re trying* is discontinuous.

From these illustrations the reader will readily be able to construct clauses on different patterns, such as S A P A, A S P, A S P C C A A, P C, P C A. The patterns themselves conform to a pattern. For instance, S occurs no more than once in each clause; C no more than twice consecutively; S either precedes P, or follows the first word in P. Many possible arrangements of S, P, C, and A are excluded as 'un-English' (except possibly in poetic usage); among them are P C S ('Scratched me he'); C A A P ('Him quickly to me send'); C C S P ('Me the book you sent'). To give a description of the English clause, or any other unit, it is necessary both to list the elements which are the building blocks of the pattern, and to state the rules which determine their relative positions, together with what omissions and repetitions are allowed.

Although this is no place for a detailed justification of this plan of description, some reasons for abandoning traditional terms and categories ought to be supplied. The old method of clause parsing, using the two objects, indirect object, etc., could not handle satisfactorily the type of clause here characterised as having more than one predicator: S P P C ('I want to do it'); S P Z P C ('I want him to do it'); etc. The elements object and complement were not shown to have a common relation to the 'verb'. 'Verb' itself was a misleading term in clause analysis, as it was easily confused with 'verb' as a part of speech, or even with 'verb' as a type of word-stem; so the distinction was unclear between a sequence of words 'has been trying', and one word in that sequence (*trying*), and a part of that word (*try-*). A rank-based description avoids these confusions, because of the insistence that each sentence should be fully described at all ranks. Informally, 'the dog had it' might be parsed as a sentence made up of a subject 'the dog', a verb 'had', and an object 'it'. But to be precise, the sentence consists of a single clause S P C, and of the three groups at S, P, and C, that at S consists of two words, and those at P and C consist of one.

Class

No account of language is possible without a classification of items by their similarities and differences. Noun, verb, preposition, etc., are classes of word (parts of speech); affirmative, imperative, and interrogative are clause classes. These are some of many familiar traditional names for grammatical classes in English. Units are assigned to classes on a number of grounds:

(*a*) Their function in the next largest unit.

Prepositions are a class of word which occur in initial position in a type of adverbial group, the 'prepositional phrase'.

(*b*) Their structure.

Affirmative clauses are marked by a structure containing the sequence s p, where p is a finite predicator.

(*c*) The way they combine with other units of the same rank.

The rule of number concord states that a singular verbal group at p presupposes a singular nominal group at s. This is part of the definition of the 'singular' class of verbal group.

Each of these criteria has to be given its due weight in the analysis of language, but the first, or functional criterion has priority in descriptive statements, because the whole notion of structure is founded on it. Each element of structure is associated with a specific class of the next smallest unit. In clause structure, the NOMINAL GROUP is that type of group which operates at s and c; the VERBAL GROUP operates at p; the ADVERBIAL GROUP operates at a. The separation of groups into these three classes is the most important classification for this unit. Classes distinguished in this way are called PRIMARY.

System

Classification presupposes some relative notion of sameness and contrast. By SYSTEMS, or sets of classes in contrast, we break primary classes into finer, more precise categories (SECONDARY CLASSES), and define the conditions under which one class is selected rather than another. The broad class 'noun' is subdivided by such systems as mass/countable; concrete/ abstract; singular/plural; animate/inanimate; personal/impersonal. A choice from one system may depend on a choice from another: for example, all mass nouns are singular. As a description becomes more detailed, more and more choices have to be recognised. At a moderate degree of refinement, we would distinguish a class of plural personal nouns (or in full, concrete-countable-plural-animate-personal nouns) *people, boys, aunts, journalists, . . .*, etc. The choices are not always binary:

the system of person for pronouns and verbs has three terms – first person, second person, and third person.

Secondary Classes and Structures

Corresponding to secondary classes are SECONDARY STRUCTURES, which result from a finer discrimination of structural patterns, and the classes which can operate in them. The interdependence of secondary classes and secondary structures can be clarified by two related examples.

Cases of secondary structures are the traditional clause types 'subject+ verb+complement', 'subject+verb+object', 'subject+verb+indirect-object+object', 'subject+verb+object+object-complement'. To distinguish these, in the present framework, we need two sets of secondary elements: P^t (transitive predicator) and P^l (linking predicator: based on the verb *to be* or one that can be used equivalently, such as *stay, feel, become*); c^o (object) and c^c (complement in the traditional sense). The four types of clauses can then be represented as follows (excluding possible adjuncts):

s P^l c^c	*'subject+verb+complement'*
s P^t c^o	*'subject+verb+object'*
s P^t c^o c^o	*'subject+verb+indirect-object+object'*
s P^t c^o c^c	*'subject+verb+object+object-complement'*

As implied in these formulae, the difference between c^o and c^c is a matter of co-occurrence: P^l is always followed by c^c, and P^t by c^o. As secondary elements in clause structure, however, they relate to secondary classes of the nominal group, which we will call NOUN GROUP and ADJECTIVE GROUP since they have a noun and an adjective respectively as their main (obligatory) elements. The noun group can act as s, c^o, or c^c, but the adjective group acts only as c^c; in other words, c^c is the only element at which the choice between a noun and an adjective group is open. The alternatives are illustrated here in the two secondary structures containing c^c:

s P^l c^c	He felt *an idiot*	(noun group)
	He felt *equal to the job*	(adjective group)
s P^t c^o c^c	He made her *his wife*	(noun group)
	He made her *mad*	(adjective group)

We turn now to nominal group structure, to see how noun groups, adjective groups, and other types of nominal group are differentiated by secondary structures. The primary structure of the nominal group has three elements x (pre-modifier), H (head), and Y (post-modifier). The possible combinations of these elements in a noun group are summarised in the formula (x . . .) H (Y . . .), in which dots indicate any number of repetitions of x and Y, and brackets indicate that these elements are optional. This formula allows for such structures as H ('people'), x H ('the person'), H Y Y ('prices here in London'), x x x H Y ('the finest woollen carpets in the world'). The class of word at H is a noun; at x, a very general class of words operates, which we will call the 'pre-noun'; Y will be ignored at this stage. The pre-noun is broken down into four chief secondary classes, determiner (*the, this, all, many*, etc.); numeral (*ten, third,* etc.); adjective (*best, lovely,* etc.); and a certain range of nouns, including proper names and words denoting substances (for example, *Westminster* in 'Westminster Bridge', and *gold* in 'gold watch'). These classes have a preferred order of occurrence in the nominal group, which is the order in which they have just been listed. To represent this order in structure, x is replaced by four secondary elements, D (for determiners), O (for numerals), E (for adjectives), and N (for nouns). In this new, more detailed form of statements, groups of the primary structure x x x x H will be represented differently:

D   DE   E   H
such a delicious spongy mixture

D   O E   N   H
all ten fabulous winter cruises

D   E   E   E   H
the finest hand-woven woollen carpets

Subdivisions of the pre-modifier do not stop here, for there are further restrictions of order and co-occurrence. Comparatives and superlatives, for example, generally precede other adjectives; and the determiners *all, both,* and *half* precede other determiners.

The structure of the nominal group is further complicated by an additional optional place, the sub-modifier (s), which is filled by adverbs of degree and quality (*very, really, almost,* etc.) and can precede a pre-modifier, a post-modifier, or another sub-modifier. So in full, the summary structure of the noun group is ((s...) x)... H ((s...) Y)... Other secondary classes, which have a pre-modifier but no head, are exemplified by:

I didn't ask for *all these*	(D D)
Just ten of them came	(S O Y)
He's *too clever for words*	(S E Y)
Most of their furniture is *reproduction*	(N)

The adjective group, illustrated by the third of these examples, is the class of nominal group which contains E, but no H.

Some Clause Systems

To show how the concepts of class and system apply to a particular unit of English grammar, I shall introduce some of the clause systems of English.* Braces join together the classes which are terms of the same system, and each class name is followed by an example.

System of Dependence

{Independent (or main) clause	'It's a natural food'
{Dependent (or subordinate) clause	'Because it's a natural food'

Further classification of dependent clauses distinguishes 'adverbial' clauses, relative clauses, reporting clauses, etc.

Major/Minor System

{Major clause	'It's a natural food'
{Minor clause	'When still warm'

The minor clause has no predicator, so the list of its elements is S, C, A instead of S, P, C, A. But as the two nominal elements S and C are structurally differentiated by their relation to P, a nominal element in minor clauses very often cannot be identified as S or C, and has the neutral status symbolised 'z'. This is not the case with the given clause 'When still warm', which can be assigned the structure A A C, because *warm*, an adjective group, cannot be selected at S. Here are some minor clauses whose structure is represented in terms of A and z:

Once a thief, always a thief.	(A Z, A Z)
This century has brought change – *in many ways, pro-*	
bably a change for the better.	(A A Z)

---

* The extended meaning of 'clause' in this section originates in as yet unpublished work on English grammar by M. A. K. Halliday and J. McH. Sinclair. The Survey of English Usage (Director, Randolph Quirk) employs a similar category, but prefers the term 'construction' to 'clause'.

A careful spender, he rarely took advantage of the financial
    privileges of his office.   (z)
With this in mind, he decided to wait for the return of our
    advance party.   (A Z A)

Allowing a type of clause which has no predicator is a break with traditional grammar. But the type of construction exemplified above has
the phonological and orthographic signs of clause status (for example, it is
bounded in writing by punctuation marks), and intuition tells us that it is
equivalent to a clause in function and meaning. Further evidence of the
need for a major/minor system in the grammatical description of English
will emerge in later chapters: it is the key to some problems which arise
in the description of the grammar of advertising.

Finite/Non-finite System

{ Finite clause   'It's a natural food'
{ Non-finite clause   'Being a natural food'

This system applies only to major clauses, as the difference between the
two classes lies in the presence of a finite or non-finite verbal group at the
first P of the clause. In full, therefore, the classes should be entitled
'finite predicator clause' and 'non-finite predicator clause'. The types of
verbal group designated 'non-finite' are those based on the infinitive or
participial forms of the verb. The most common types of non-finite
clause have no subject; the example above has the structure P C.

System of Mood

{ Affirmative clause   'It's a natural food'
{ Interrogative clause   'Is it a natural food?'
{ Imperative clause   'Try some'.

Little need be said about this system, as it fits fairly closely the well understood distinction between statements, questions, and commands (which
are, however, contextual rather than grammatical categories). The system
of mood applies only to independent clauses. Interrogative clauses divide
into '*Yes/No* interrogatives' (those which demand a positive or negative
answer) and '*Wh-* interrogatives', which begin with a question word
such as *who, what, why, how*.

How do these systems fit together? Any given clause is the product of
selections from all four of them, but not all selections are independent of

one another. 'It's a natural food', which has served to illustrate the first term of each system, is in full an 'independent-major-finite-affirmative clause'. However, the shorter designation 'affirmative clause' will do just as well, as 'affirmative' implies 'independent' and 'finite', and 'finite' in its turn implies 'major'.

Depth-ordered Structure

Up to this point, the idea of linguistic structure has been based on the principle of PLACE-ORDERING: the principle whereby the order in which the elements of a pattern occur is tied to the class of unit they represent. Thus the meaning of H in a group structure X H Y is not merely that of 'second element in a sequence of three', but that of an element standing for a particular word class, the noun. But we also have to accommodate the principle of recursive structure, or DEPTH-ORDERING in language.*
Depth-ordering means that the elements of a sequence are not distinguished from one another on the basis of class membership, but simply by their position relative to one another (which could be represented, for example, by numbering the elements 1, 2, 3,... in order). Such a recursive pattern is said to have a 'depth' of x, where x is the number of elements it contains. Depth-ordering was acknowledged earlier in the use of dots after an element to signify the possibility of repetitions (x..., s...). However, it is best treated as a separate structural dimension, or rather set of structural dimensions, interacting in different ways with the type of structure so far considered.

The three types, or dimensions of depth-ordered structure are:

CO-ORDINATION: 'Twelve lords a-leaping, eleven ladies dancing, ...three French hens, two turtle doves, and a partridge in a pear tree.'

DEPENDENCE: 'I sensed that he sensed that I sensed...that he sensed that I was lying.'

EMBEDDING: 'I know a man who knows a man...who knows a man who will do it for nothing.'

The first of these examples is part of the last verse of the song *The Twelve Days of Christmas*; in full, it has the unusual depth of twelve. The other two examples are also freakish, not only because of their contextual implausibility, but because any sequence of these types with a depth of

---

* See Halliday (1963b).

2—E.I.A.

more than three or four would be exceptional. But in principle no maximum can be placed on the number of units which may make up a depth-ordered structure. In this, the freakishness of the examples has an illustrative value; for long as they are, they could be expanded indefinitely by the insertion of more and more elements of the same kind at the point where dots have been printed.

Co-ordination

Under this heading are included:

> LINKING: 'No need to worry about *spotty pans, soiled paintwork, or grease stains.*'
> (Noun group linking; depth – 3)
> APPOSITION: 'This is *Abel Summers, the well-known folk singer.*'
> (Noun group apposition; depth – 2)
> PARATAXIS: 'And it's now *bigger; crisper; more nourishing than ever before.*'
> (Adjective group parataxis; depth – 3)

Linking means that the elements are joined by an initial co-ordinating conjunction (*and, or, but*) on the last element, or on every one except the first. The relationship of apposition between elements is marked in speech by tone-concord, or equivalent intonation patterns on each element. Semantically, it signifies an equative or attributive relation. In parataxis, as in apposition, there is no linking word. There may be tone-concord (rising or falling), or on the other hand there may be the kind of 'listing' contour which often occurs with linking – that is, the voice rises on each element except the last, on which it falls. Parataxis has the same enumerative semantic function as linking.

Mostly the elements of a co-ordinative structure are units of the same rank and class. But there is also a type of co-ordination, BRANCHING, which operates on parts of units. It is most common in the post-subjectival part of a clause: 'She has good taste, and knows her own mind' (s p c/p c). Here the subject is shared by both clauses, and both predicators agree with it in number and person.

Dependence

Dependence is the type of depth-ordering that accounts for repetitions in place-ordered structure. Subordination in sentences is a familiar example. There are only two places of sentence structure: m 'main' (for independent clauses) and s 'subordinate' (for dependent clauses). Every sentence contains an independent clause, and any number of subordinate clauses optionally precede, follow, or interrupt it. This is expressed in the formula (s...) M ⟨(s...)⟩ (s...). However, what actually underlies the recursive symbol s... is the observation that any dependent clause may itself have a further dependent clause depending on it. In a sentence of the structure M S S , the relationship between s and s is the same as that which obtains between M and S, although in the latter case it coincides with a difference of primary class. So on this structural formula may be imposed a further notation *a, b, c*, indicating depth and direction of dependence (where *a* is the independent clause):

M*a*	s*b*	s*c*
I knew	that you had seen him	before I met you.

This case, where the dependence relation goes from left to right is called PROGRESSIVE DEPENDENCE, whereas the opposite case (right to left) is REGRESSIVE or anticipatory dependence. More than one clause can be dependent on the same clause. The sentence above is in fact ambiguous, and under another interpretation can be analysed:

M*a*	s*b*	s*b*
I knew	that you had seen him	before I met you.

where both the second and third clauses depend on the first. This is now equivalent in meaning to:

s*b*	M*a*	s*b*
Before I met you,	I knew	that you had seen him.

a sentence which contains both regressive and progressive dependence.

Modification in the nominal group is another important case of dependence. In a noun group, the head is the independent element, the pre-modifier and post-modifier correspond to *b*, and the sub-modifier to *c, d, e,....*

x*b*	x*b*		x*b*	x*b*	H*a*
such	wonderful	new	washable		materials

s*e*	s*d*	s*c*	x*b*	H*a*
very	much	more	expensive	shirts

Embedding

The third type of depth-ordered structure is defined in terms of rank. Units ordered on the rank scale so that each unit except the lowest consists of units of the rank next below: so a sentence consists of one or more clauses, a clause of one or more groups, etc. But this does not exclude a recursive application of the ranking relation, such that (for example) a group may occur within a group, or a clause within a clause. By '*x* is within *y*', we are to understand a specific relation, namely '*x* operates at an element in *y*'s structure'. EMBEDDING* is a shift in rank, whereby a group acts as a word, or a word acts as a morpheme, etc. In the nominal group, the post-modifier is almost always a place for embedded structure. The prepositional phrase in 'a pipeful of good tobacco' is an embedded adverbial group, and 'good tobacco' in turn is a nominal group within the adverbial group. So here already there is embedding to a depth of 3: a group within a group within a group. It may be shown like this:

Nominal group:	D H	Y	I.
Adverbial group:		P C	2.
Nominal group:		E H	3.

a pipeful of good tobacco

Or more simply by bracketing:

(a pipeful (of (good tobacco)))

The following more complex nominal group contains embedding to a depth of 5:

(the chance (of (a holiday (in (the Mediterranean)))))

The principle of embedding extends to the 'demotion' of a unit by more than one rank. A defining relative clause such as 'the best *you can buy*' is a clause which enters into nominal group structure as a post-modifier, and therefore has the status of a word. The nominal genitive is another case of double rank shift:

(((Mary)'s aged grandmother)'s faithful servant)

The nominal groups 'Mary' and 'Mary's aged grandmother' act as morphemes: as stems to which the genitive suffix spelt 's is added to make up a determiner, structurally equivalent to *its*, *his*, etc.

---

* Halliday's term is 'rank-shift'. In other theories of language, 'embedding' has been used in a sense approximately covering both dependence and rank-shift; e.g. in Jerrold J. Katz and Paul M. Postal, *An Integrated Theory of Linguistic Descriptions* (Cambridge, Mass., 1964), p. 12.

Phonology, Orthography, Vocabulary

There will be no need to go into detail on the description of English at levels other than grammar. The patterns of phonology and orthography, although less complex than those of grammar, are susceptible to a similar type of analysis, using the concepts of unit, structure, class, and system. In phonology we recognise four units; in decreasing order, they are TONE GROUP (unit of intonation), FOOT (unit of rhythm), SYLLABLE, and PHONEME.* The tone group's structure is stated as (Pretonic...) Tonic..., and the beginning of the tonic part marks the 'climax' or NUCLEUS of the pattern, where the most significant changes of pitch take place. Different tones, or movements of pitch, constitute a system fall/high rise/low rise/ fall+rise/rise+fall. The falling tone is associated with finality and affirmation, whereas the rising tone is that generally used on *Yes/No* questions. The low rise implies lack of finality, and is used, for example, on anticipatory dependent clauses. It is less easy to generalise about the functions of the other two tones.

The units of orthography include the letter, the orthographic word, the orthographic sentence, and the paragraph. The qualification 'orthographic' here is not mere pedantry, for it must be insisted that the units of orthography are not, any more than those of phonology, in a one-to-one relation with grammatical units. Grammatical categories are defined grammatically: that is, by their relation to other grammatical categories. Hence the presence or absence of a space between two strings of letters should not be used as a criterion for deciding what is and what is not a word in grammar. Recalling the inconsistences and idiosyncrasies in the use of the hyphen, we can see that such a criterion would lead to impossible analyses. However, there are cases, such as apposition and parataxis, where phonology and orthography provide essential clues for the *recognition* of grammatical distinctions.

The principles of rank and structure do not apply to lexis in the same sense as to the other levels. But here again there is need to emphasise the independence of the categories of one level from those of another. The dictionary is commonly held to be a book about words: but since 'word' has already been used to designate a grammatical category, it will be preferable to use a different label, LEXICAL ITEM, for the units of vocabulary which are the subject matter of lexicography. In most cases, the two categories coincide. But there are thousands of examples of lexical items composed of a sequence of words: *put out* (='extinguish'), *take a liking to*,

---

* See Halliday (1963a), pp. 5–8, 10.

central heating, district nurse, it never rains but it pours, etc. Conversely, *the, and, for, someone, are,* etc., are 'grammatical words' which, except when they are part of idioms, can be best formally characterised in terms of their grammatical, rather than lexical, functions. Idioms are treated as multi-word lexical items not only because they are semantically indivisible (in the sense that their meaning is not the conjunction of the meaning of their parts), but because they act as single 'blocks' in the formal structure of language. In 'I won't put up with this behaviour', the significant parts of the lexical structure are 'put up with' and 'behaviour', which together make up a COLLOCATION or co-occurrence of lexical items. It can be seen from this example that collocations, the basic structural components of lexical patterning, may cut right across structural divisions of grammar.

Part One Advertising English and
Other Englishes

Chapter 3

Language and Motive

When the word 'advertising' is mentioned, most of us automatically think of what might be more accurately called 'commercial consumer advertising': advertising directed towards a mass audience with the aim of promoting sales of a commercial product or service. This is the most important type, but others come easily to mind. 'Trade' advertising in trade journals is addressed to the retailer by the manufacturer or distributor. Retail advertising is addressed to the potential customer by the retailer. 'Prestige' advertising is on the borders of advertising and public relations: it seeks not so much to promote sales, as to bring about an alignment of public opinion with commercial interests. Some advertising is initiated not by commercial enterprise but by governmental departments and non-profit-making bodies such as charities. And, of course, the 'classifieds' in national and local publications are often initiated by private individuals.

It is not easy to say what is in common between these various types of publicity without including others to which the word 'advertising' would be hesitantly applied. Is a theatre bill or a package label an advertisement? What about the butcher's price-tag 'Only 3/4 per lb', or the notice in his window 'Smart lad wanted'? Taking decisions in these cases is arbitrary and pointless. Let us simply observe that 'advertising' covers a whole range of situations, which shade off vaguely into such neighbouring areas as public announcements, public relations, and public polemics.

Commercial consumer advertising is the kind which uses most money, professional skill, and advertising space in this country. It includes almost all television advertising. It is the natural centre of focus for a book on advertising, and I shall adhere to the convenient usage of popular custom, by letting 'advertising' mean 'commercial consumer advertising' unless there is something special to be said about the other types.

Most advertising language comes under the broader heading of 'loaded language'; that is, it aims to change the will, opinions, or attitudes of its audience (whether in the interests of the audience or not is a separate matter). Advertising differs from other types of loaded language (such as political journalism and religious oratory) in having a very precise material goal. Changing the mental disposition of the audience is only important in so far as it leads to the desired kind of behaviour – buying a particular kind of product. And in normal competitive conditions this means buying brand A rather than equivalent brands B, C, or D. The goal could scarcely be more specific.

A number of other general differences between the advertising situation and other loaded language situations need to be mentioned, although some of them are obvious enough.

1. An advertisement is of necessity honest in declaring its purpose. The mention of the brand-name is usually sufficient to identify an advertisement for what it is, and, in addition, regulations at least partially safeguard the public against camouflaged advertising.
2. The advertiser has to buy his way to the public's attention; budgeting economy of means against results, in terms of sales returns, is an especially important consideration for him.
3. Whereas other forms of persuasion can expect to meet with interested responses varying from active support to active hostility, the average person's attitude to advertising is bored tolerance, mixed with varying degrees of good or ill-humour.
4. Advertising uses a predominantly concrete language, matching its concrete purpose. Propagandists in other fields tend to deal in abstractions.
5. Elsewhere appeals are often made to moral and ethical principles; advertising largely confines itself to basic human drives such as gain, emulation, protectiveness, and the physical appetites.

The most straightforward kind of advertisement is one which describes what special need the product fulfils, or what special advantage it offers. The trouble with this approach in a competitive market is that it tends to lead to a vicious circle of innovation, in which inordinate claims are made for the sake of 'news value'. Each advertiser tries to steal a march over his competitors by publicising the most trivial change in his product as a vast improvement. In addition, for many products it is often difficult to think of any material quality which could be given as a reason for preferring one brand to another. Consequently, in recent years an alternative 'brand-image' approach,* which aims to establish a stable market over a long period, has grown in importance. It is often more practicable to

---

* A well-known investigation of the cult of the 'brand-image' in American advertising is Packard (1957), especially Chapter 5.

represent a product in a way which will identify it with popular desires than to *persuade* the public into liking it.

To be a success, a typical advertisement must accomplish four things in sequence:

1. It must draw attention to itself.
2. It must sustain the interest it has attracted.
3. It must be remembered, or at any rate recognised as familiar.
4. It must prompt the right kind of action.

Advertising opinion varies on the relative importance of these pre-requisites, and on the role which language plays in fulfilling them. According to one extreme position, copy counts for little. 'What you say doesn't matter, so long as you hammer the brand-name into their heads.' Present testing methods cannot disprove this assertion.* But whatever its merits, many characteristics of advertising language can be directly related to one of the four principles listed. They can be considered under the respective headings of ATTENTION VALUE, READABILITY (or 'listenability'), MEMORABILITY, and SELLING POWER.

Attention Value

Whatever medium is used, advertising usually competes at a great disadvantage with other claims on the public's attention. The means of overcoming this disadvantage belong more often to other means of communication or to the transmission of language than to language itself: illustration, display typography, vocal emphasis, and so on. But one way of provoking the consumer's attention and curiosity is to present him with something surprising and unexpected, and this can be done as well by the unorthodox use of language as by other means. Any kind of unconventional behaviour, linguistic or otherwise, compels notice. The copywriter who exploits this fact can be compared to a legendary customer in a crowded restaurant, who stood on his head to attract the waiter's attention.

Departing from the conventions or rules of language can take many forms, and some of them will be examined in Chapters 20 and 22. In its grossest form, it is a violation of some obvious rule of the language: perhaps a 'wrong' spelling, or a grammatical solecism. Because this type of

---

* What is called 'copy testing' in advertising research is a test not of isolated linguistic features but of the gross effectiveness of a slogan or of the entire copy of an advertisement. See, for example, Weir (1960), pp. 125–9.

unorthodoxy usually carries penalties of misunderstanding or disapproval, it is the least important variety of unconventionality. Neologism (inventing new words) is another type which requires tactful handling. But there is considerable scope for inventiveness in the two areas of semantics and context. Semantic unorthodoxy can be crudely characterised as 'playing with the meanings of words', and is the basis of many linguistic jokes and some important literary devices such as metaphor and paradox. Contextual unorthodoxy consists in exploiting the incongruity of language in an inappropriate situation.

Readability

How to ensure that attentiveness continues after the bait has been taken? On a psychological plane, this might mean 'how to keep up suspense, interest, or amusement'. On a linguistic plane, it is more a question of how to make the message easy to grasp and assimilate. Some efforts have been made to assess objectively the 'readability' of written language, by measuring the simplicity of its structure in combination with other factors, or by finding out how easy it is to predict individual words from their environments.* The latter measure conflicts with attention value and interest value, which place a premium on the unexpected and enigmatic, as opposed to the predictable. But the conflict does not arise if, as often happens in press advertising, the surprise element is concentrated in the headline.

'Readability' has, unfortunately, no ready terminological equivalent for spoken language. However, the properties which make language easy to read are basically the same as those which make it easy to listen to. The basic requirements are a simple, personal, and colloquial style, and a familiar vocabulary. What is involved in the terms 'simple', 'personal', and 'colloquial' will be seen in Chapter 8.

Memorability

Advertising has to make a lasting impression if it is to affect buying behaviour. But a conscious and detailed memory of an individual advertisement is usually too high an objective to aim at.† It is more

---

* See Flesch (1951), and Taylor (1953), pp. 415–33.

† On recall testing in advertising, see Harris and Seldon (1962), pp. 129–32.

through being repeatedly subjected to a particular advertisement, or to an advertising campaign, or to an advertising programme extending over a long period, that a consumer becomes and stays familiar with the product, and the virtues which are claimed for it.)

Memorability of language can be more or less equated with 'memorisability'. Verbatim recall is the very highest goal to which a copywriter could aspire, and in general it is obviously beyond what he requires or can achieve. Yet an advertisement gains nothing unless the name of the product is remembered, so at least in this respect, it is desirable that part of the linguistic message should be memorised. In fact the role of the verbal memory extends beyond the brand-name, to the memorising of slogans, key phrases, snatches of song, etc. By dint of repetition, whether in a single commercial or a whole advertising campaign, the consumer may be brought to the point where the brand-name and some catch-phrase associated with it are mutual recall stimuli, so that the product is, so to speak, stored in his mind with a permanently attached label.

(Repetition obviously plays an essential role in memorisation. (The amount of repetition of both spoken and printed advertising is phenomenal, and has a bearing on certain peculiarities of advertising syntax (see especially the discussion of iteration on pp. 147–8).)One apparent drawback is that it may tend to bore or infuriate the consumer, according to his temperament. But the advertising world is unconcerned about this: it has yet to be shown that hostility of some consumers to the advertising significantly affects the disposition of others to buy the product.

It is a general principle that if a piece of language is repeated often enough, it will stick. But a more interesting question is 'What makes one piece of language intrinsically more memorable than another?'(To some extent, the ease with which we remember a thing depends on the impact it first made on us; in this respect, the goal of memorability coincides with that of attention value. But there are other aids to memory, such as the phonological regularities of alliteration, metrical rhythm, and rhyme. These are features which make verse easier to memorise than prose, and which make the jingle perhaps the most powerful mnemonic device in advertising. They are discussed in Chapter 21, together with the grammatical device of parallelism, which probably also has mnemonic value.

Selling Power

Here we reach the crucial and most mysterious part of the advertising process. Whether copy sells or not is its criterion of success; yet there is no satisfactory way of finding out what general linguistic features, if any, contribute to this objective. To take an obvious example, one of the most striking features of the grammar of advertising is an extreme frequency of imperative clauses. The consumer is for ever being told to 'get' this, 'buy' that, 'taste' the other. But there is no evidence that these direct exhortations, however importunate, get results. It is within human experience that telling someone to do something is less successful than politely *asking* him to do it, or even asking him *not* to do it.

One can plausibly deny that there is any general connection between language and selling power. In fact it is not easy to generalise about any properties of advertisements that sell. Success depends on many known and unknown variables, not the least of which is the unanalysable creative skill of choosing and implementing the right kind of selling approach for the right kind of situation. The kernel of the sales message – the 'vital promise' or 'unique selling proposition' – has to be in some way special and different for each product. It would seem vain to look for uniformity in an area where uniqueness is held in honour.

To take this negative position too seriously, however, would be to resign from the most challenging part of relating language to situation. The three principles of attention value, readability, and memorability explains by no means all the standard features of advertising language. It seems reasonable that others should be explained as those which have been found by experience or instinct to have virtue in selling. The alternative would be to consider them valueless conventions which somehow, through habit or tradition, have become part of the copywriter's stock-in-trade. We cannot ultimately prove their usefulness, nor should we ignore the element of conservatism in copywriting practice. But when forms of language seem to have a clear motivation in terms of selling tactics, there is no harm in pointing it out.

Moreover, a novel or unique claim on behalf of a product does not have to be expressed in novel language. It is no paradox that some of the commonest advertising clichés put emphasis on the uniqueness of the advertised product: 'Nothing else; 'No other'; 'there's nothing like'; 'the best in the world'; 'Britain's best'; 'the best you can buy'; or simply 'the best' The hyperbolic character of advertising language, as shown, for example, in the unstinted use of superlatives, relates on the one hand to the desirability of a unique claim on behalf of the product, and on the other hand to the principle (asserted in every copywriting textbook) that an advertising message should be positive and unreserved. Compromises, half-measures and discouraging negatives are avoided. (One exception to this is the use of negatives in phrases such as 'no other' cited above, which are emphatic disclaimers of the equality of competing brands.) 'Be positive' carries the implication 'Be laudatory'; as claims about the advertised commodity and its consumption are calculated to commend it to the consumer, any derogatory reference presupposes a negative approach – 'This is *not* what the product is like', 'This is *not* how the consumer feels', etc. Several obvious features of advertising language can be attributed to this principle: the infrequency of prohibitions and negative forms generally; the great frequency of approbatory adjectives, and the corresponding infrequency of disapprobatory ones; the frequency of unqualified comparatives (simply 'better' rather than 'better than x'). Part II of the book considers such features in more detail, together with many others which have a less obvious connection with the selling motive.

Chapter 4

The Advertising Situation

We have considered the advertising situation informally, from the point of view of advertising strategy. Let us now look at it in a way which will serve as a framework for linguistic description.

A gross description of any situation of linguistic communication is obtained from answers to the following questions:

    1. Who are the participants?
    2. What objects are relevant to the communication?
    3. What is the medium of communication?
    4. What is the purpose or effect of communication?*

To enlarge upon these:

    1. By participants, I mean first person (speaker/writer), second person (listener/reader), and any third persons involved (for example, the audience in a debate or music-hall turn). First person, second person, and third person are here categories of people involved in the language situation; they do not always correspond to the grammatical categories of first, second, and third person pronouns. For example, *you* is a second person pronoun, but in a sentence like 'They treat you like dirt', it is used indefinitely, to include all categories of participants in the situation.

    2. What objects are relevant to a situation depends, of course, on the interpretation we give to 'relevant'. As a rough guide, we might use a combination of the following criteria: (*a*) whether it is mentioned or discussed, (*b*) whether it is physically or sensibly present; (*c*) whether it is involved in the purpose or effect of the communication.

    3. The most important distinction of medium is between auditory and visual communication, or (if the terms are understood widely enough) between *speech* and *writing*. But under this heading we also specify artificial media such as the telephone, print, radio, and tele-

---

* This scheme is roughly based on that of Firth (1957), p. 182.

vision; and special kinds of vocal delivery such as chanting and sing-
ing.

4. The different implications of 'purpose' and 'effect' may not be of
consequence. Advertising is one of those situations for which it is
easier to concentrate on purpose: the effect of advertising may take a
multitude of individual forms, and may be only partly a question of
buying or not buying the product; but the purpose remains fairly
constant, and is easily describable.

To illustrate this framework of description, I shall take a familiar
domestic situation (familiar, at least, as a theme of popular humour).

THE SITUATION OF THE 'BACK-SEAT DRIVER'

1. *Participants:* A. Wife (first person).
                   B. Husband (second person).
2. *Relevant object:* a car.
3. *Medium:* speech.
4. *Purpose:* to control B's driving of 2.

If there are other passengers in the car, they might be considered third
person participants. They would be relevant to the situation if they
affected A's manner of speaking to B.

Now to describe at its most general a situation within the present
field of study:

COMMERCIAL TELEVISION ADVERTISING

1. *Participants:* A. Advertiser (first person).
                   B. Consumer (second person).
2. *Relevant object:* a product.
3. *Medium:* television; speech and writing.
4. *Purpose:* to promote sales of 2 to B.

When we move from a situation of private communication to one of
public communication, we encounter complications. At both the initiating and the receiving ends of the message, a large number of people may
be involved. 'Consumer' here is a coverall term for a vast audience often
running into millions. The 'advertiser' is not a single person, but an
abstract assemblage of people: the organisation which commissions and
pays for the advertising. The process of originating the message is particularly complex in television advertising. The advertiser usually dele-

gates the work of preparing advertising policy and advertising campaigns to an agency. It is possible that one man in the agency (a copywriter) may be responsible for the composition of the verbal message; but what he writes will be subject to approval and modification by others. Finally, the agency delegates the making of the television film (possibly with further modifications of the script) to a filming company; and the people actually speaking the message will frequently themselves be independent practitioners. All are ultimately working for, and answerable to, the advertiser, who must therefore be considered the initiator of the message, although he may take little part in its actual composition and production.

One further complication in the advertising situation can be appreciated after a moment's reflection on the variety of roles language may be required to play in it. Although on one level the participants are advertiser and consumer, on another level many kinds of SECONDARY PARTICIPANTS enter into the situation. The public is addressed by celebrities, 'ordinary housewives', cartoon characters, even talking animals, who in one way or another testify to the merits of the product. Secondary participants also enter into discourse with one another: for example, in interviews and dramatised domestic dialogues. There is also a category of third person secondary participants: people who are pictured and talked about in the advertisement, although they do not actually say anything.

As we define a linguistic situation with reference to its participants, the notion of secondary participants brings with it the notion of SECONDARY SITUATIONS, which are in a sense included within the PRIMARY SITUATION. In television commercials, the events pictured on the screen, together with the speech of people depicted on the screen, constitute the secondary situation. The distinction can be thought of as an opposition between the advertising situation itself and the situations which are created within it; or, from a different point of view, between that which is the common ground of advertisements generally, and that which varies from advertisement to advertisement.

On this basis I shall distinguish between the language of DIRECT ADDRESS advertising, for which both first and second persons are primary participants, and that of INDIRECT ADDRESS advertising in which the advertising message reaches the consumer through the mouths of secondary participants. The most important division in indirect address advertising is between MONOLOGUE and DIALOGUE. In the former, a secondary participant addresses the consumer; in the latter, both first and second persons are secondary participants. There is one constant feature in both primary and almost all secondary situations: the presence and relevance of the product. The differences and similarities between them can be set out like this:

	1st Person	2nd Person	Relevant Object
Direct Address	advertiser	consumer	product
Indirect Address			
Monologue	secondary participant	consumer	product
Dialogue	secondary participant	secondary participant	product

It will be seen in Chapter 5 that degrees of affinity in language correspond to the extent to which the situations themselves are similar. At this stage it is sufficient to quote 30-second commercials which illustrate the three types:

1. *Direct Address*

   Inside this can is a meal so tasty you might have made it yourself. It's the new Fray Bentos Steak and Kidney Pie. Your butcher couldn't sell you better meat. Prime, lean steak...tender kidney... in good rich meaty gravy – and capped by lovely, light, crispy pastry. A meal like this sets a man up! The new Fray Bentos Steak and Kidney Pie.*

2. *Indirect Address: Monologue*

   I'm as bad as the kids at Christmas. Eat much too much. Trouble is, at my age it shows. But my chemist has the answer to this 'Christmas Spread'. Metercal. With Metercal you can count on losing at least half a pound a day. Mark you, it's not just a slimming product. It's a complete and balanced diet food. So you never get hungry while you're losing weight...And I haven't felt so fit for ages. So if your waist-band is feeling a bit tight after Christmas – try Metercal.

3. *Indirect Address: Dialogue*

   Interviewer: Excuse me, can I by any chance...
   Girl: Oh you certainly could, it's terribly heavy.

---

* This and all other quotations from television scripts will be given with approximately the original punctuation. Some changes are necessary where the script punctuation, because of the lay-out of the text in columns opposite visual directions, would look strange in running text and would not give clear enough indications of grammatical structure.

Interviewer: Oh yes, of course. But actually I just wanted to ask you about Polo Mint.

Girl: Polo! Oh they're lovely.

Interviewer: Oh good!

Girl: They're so clean tasting and refreshing; handy for my bag too and they've got a hole in the middle.

Interviewer: I'm terribly sorry.

Girl: And they're lovely and minty. Would you like one?

Interviewer: Thanks very much.

Girl: Oh! My Polos.

———————————

Polo's only 2d.   Polo the mint with the hole.

The last sentence of this third example is spoken by a commentator's voice in direct address to the viewer: a return to the primary situation at the end of a commercial is common, especially following dialogue. A mixture of direct and indirect address copy in the same advertisment is not unusual, and in some advertisements this is taken to the extent of having frequent switches of situation throughout.

Secondary situations resemble the primary situation not only in having the product as their theme, but in placing focus on the consumption, rather than the production of the advertised brand. Example 1 is typical of direct address advertising in its emphasis on *you* the consumer to the exclusion of *us* the advertisers. Similarly, most secondary participants are portraits of average members of the consumer public. They might, like the speaker in example 2 or the girl in example 3 above, be enthusiastically satisfied customers, or else people caught in the act of using the product and discovering its merits. Occasional appearances are made by secondary participants involved in the production of the article, from factory hands up to managing directors. There is also a small class of secondary participants connected neither with the initiating nor the receiving end of the message. Such neutral personages are presenters, interviewers, and people who might be entitled 'objective authorities' on the product concerned: retailers, farmers, etc. However, the most common function of the secondary situations is to hold up a mirror to the consumer: to have her identify her own needs with those answered by the product, through dramatic involvement with the secondary participants.

The characterisation of the primary television advertising situation at the beginning of this chapter involved some simplifications. Thinking of advertising as typically a competitive activity, we might wonder whether rival products and advertisers should not be included as relevant objects and participants, and whether the purpose of competitive advertising should be amended to 'promotion of sales...*at the expense of other brands*'. Strictly speaking, it should, for every loaded language situation has at least an implied negative aspect. But the negative aspect is rarely stressed; 'knocking copy', designed to discredit competing products, offends against the principle of 'positiveness' mentioned earlier, and is besides considered bad form.* My picture of the advertising situation therefore reflected the simplicity of the situation as advertising practice makes it appear, and rival advertisers, if they enter into the situation at all, merely loom ghostlike in the background.

\A high proportion of press advertising copy is in direct address to the consumer; in television advertising, the proportion is more even – roughly 60 per cent to 40 per cent. Television is immensely superior to the press in making secondary participants alive and convincing, and appeal to human interest in this medium is a powerful factor in keeping the viewer's attention. Dialogue situations in particular have rich possibilities on television, whereas in the press they are largely restricted to the old-fashioned strip-cartoon story, a stand-by for one or two products but in general a device of very limited usefulness. On the other hand, one of the strengths of the press medium is its suitability to detailed explanatory copy, which is better presented directly, rather than through secondary participants.

Whenever a speaker appears on the television screen in a commercial, we may take it that he is identifiable as an individual personality, and speaks in his own right as a secondary participant. There are consequently only two ways in which direct address copy may be transmitted in commercials: by SUPERS (printed messages superimposed on the screen), and by COMMENTARIES spoken off the screen. In the scripts, the speaker of commentaries is variously designated 'commentator', 'announcer' and 'voice over'. Nothing could better symbolise the idea of the 'hidden persuader' than this anonymous, cajoling voice which invades the privacy of countless homes. During the last war, the B.B.C. helped to maintain confidence in its bulletins by having its newscasters identify themselves by name. In view of the complexity and (from the public's point of view) vagueness of an advertisement's origin, one might wonder why a similar injection of confidence is not advisable in television commentary. But perhaps the anonymity of the voice is a less serious business when the public recognises the motive behind the announcement, and does not

---

* Disparagement of rival brands is condemned by the British Code of Advertising Practice.

have to worry about whether it is being 'got at' – because it knows that it is.

Should the language of indirect address advertising be included or excluded from the subject matter of this study? Here is another case where we can accept either a narrow or a wide definition of advertising language. I shall take the same kind of decision as before, adhering to the narrower definition (= direct address advertising) except for incidental comment. The language of direct address advertising is more homogeneous than that of indirect address advertising, and is more rewarding to study, in the light of the aims set forth in my first chapter. It is also presumably of greater interest to anyone reading this book. But the language of secondary participants also has some interesting characteristics, which will be the subject of the next chapter. After that, we shall in general take advertising language to mean the language of direct address only.

Chapter 5

Direct and Indirect Address

We now explore the division between direct and indirect address further, noting its principal linguistic implications. Most of the illustrations will be taken from television advertising, where, for reasons already indicated, indirect address is more extensively used. But all the variations of secondary situation used on television may be used also in press advertising.

Direct Address Advertising

The role of language in direct address must be considered in conjunction with the other available means of communicating, especially pictorial material in print and events on the screen in television advertising. I have already mentioned the use of visual supers in commercials. This is a limited, supplementary means of linguistic communication, often used merely to underline the key parts of the spoken message. (The simultaneous transmission of *different* visual and auditory messages is generally considered bad advertising practice, because it creates a conflict between the two means of transmission.) Very few words can effectively appear on the screen at one time, so the language of supers is very elementary, consisting of short slogans, brand-names, price labels, and such like. It has much in common with the language of posters and package displays, with which it will be discussed later (pp. 90–7) under the heading of disjunctive mode of discourse.

The most important linguistic means of conveying the advertising message on television is therefore the spoken commentary. By using the word 'commentary', I have perhaps implied that the spoken part of the communication is subordinate to the visual part; that it explains or enlarges on the meaning of the events on the screen. This is one kind of relationship, but not the only kind. So that the relation between visual and auditory communication can be examined, the following three illustrations include both vision and sound components, as set out in production scripts. The first is a 45-second demonstration-type commercial, in which the spoken copy is closely co-ordinated with the visual sequence:

PICTURE	SOUND
Open on child's sticky hands opening door.	1½ seconds silence
As it closes her handmarks are revealed added to previous ones.	
	Commentator's voice over:
Dog's muddy paws jump against door and woman's soapy hand comes in – opens and closes it. Door slam.	Here's a job for...
Cut (or optical) to B.C.U. Handy Andy logo.	... Handy Andy, ...
Track back to reveal Handy Andy bottle on shelf. *Super:* 'The modern paintwork cleaner'.	... the modern paintwork cleaner!
Hand reaches in and takes bottle.	Use Handy Andy ...
Cut to pouring shot.	... straight from the bottle like this. It's so quick and easy.
Cut to cleaning shot of hand holding sponge making sweeping wipe over dirty door.	Handy Andy shifts grime from paintwork ...
Hand wipes up and down into characteristic shape (live sequence of press ad.) *Super:* 'Handy Andy shifts grime from paintwork like this'.	... like this!
Hand wipes whole screen area clean to reveal shining clean door.	No scratching or powdery smears. Your paintwork gleams as though it has just been freshly painted!

PICTURE	SOUND
Cut to repeat pouring shot. Cut to shot of stove showing grease spattered on wall surrounding.	Now see how Handy Andy straight from the bottle gets to work on a really tough job ...
C.U. hand holding sponge repeating characteristic cleaning action.	... the paintwork by your cooker. Handy Andy shifts really greasy dirt from paintwork like this!
Continue cleaning action to wipe whole screen area clean. Shining clean wall.	No scratching or powdery smears. All painted surfaces come clean with a wipe ...
Camera swings round to show whole kitchen gleaming. Woman putting Handy Andy away, child sitting in shining high-chair.	... when you put Handy Andy to work on them.
Cut to Handy Andy bottle on gleaming shelf. *Jump in words:* 'Makes paintwork come *clean quicker* and *easier*'.	Handy Andy cleans paintwork with a wipe.

Prominent in direct address advertising generally on television are items whose semantic function is to point or draw attention to events happening on the screen. They include *here, now, this,* and imperative verbs such as *look, see, watch.* In commercials such as the above, where the video demonstrates the use and effect of the product, they are doubly important. Notice the opening word *here,* the triple repetition of the phrase 'like this' and the sentence beginning 'Now see how ...' Demonstration commercials have a straightforward selling job to perform, and their copy tends to contain many representative features of advertising language. The Handy Andy advertisement is typical in its use of imperatives (*use, see*) and of second person pronouns ('*your* cooker', '*you* put'); in its repetitions (as many as seven) of the brand-name, and of other phrases ('No scratching or powdery smears'; 'straight from the bottle'; 'with a wipe').

The following thirty-second commercial again shows the close co-ordination between visual and verbal communication in demonstrative sequences; but it also illustrates, in its opening and closing passages, a looser relationship between the two:

VISION	SOUND
Shot of Kensitas pack. Cut to close up of woman smoking.	Kensitas give twice the pleasure – with extra fine cigarettes and famous name gifts.
Cut to shot of woman in kitchen. Cut to close up of woman closing pressure cooker.	Like this Prestige pressure cooker – free with Kensitas.
Cut to picnic scene. Cut to close up of woman picking up flask.	This Freezheat luxury picnic case – free with Kensitas.
Cut to shot of man shaving. Cut to close up of shaver.	And this Morphy Richards electric shaver – free with Kensitas.
Cut to shot of hands taking certificates out of pocket.	Gift certificates mount up so quickly . . .
Cut to close up of man smoking.	. . . so smoke and enjoy the finest Virginia tobacco money can buy . . .
Cut to Pack Shot.	. . . in Kensitas Extra Size and Kensitas Filter Tip.

The middle sequences, which show in turn three 'gifts', are accompanied by pieces of copy which might be regarded as captions to the visual illustrations. But at the beginning and end, the verbal message is self-sufficient to the extent that it might have served as material for a radio commercial. Here, it is the visual element that seems to have the subordinate role, supplementing the sales talk with routine shots of the brand package and of the product in use. The larger part of shorter fifteen-second commercials is often made up of such stereotyped sequences, and in seven-second commercials there is little time to show anything except a title card or a 'pack shot' establishing a visual image of the product. This script further exemplifies those omnipresent features of direct address copy noticed in the previous example or in earlier quotations: the imperative ('*smoke* and *enjoy* . . .'), the repetition of the brand-name and of other sections of copy, and the intensified superlative ('the finest Virginia tobacco money can buy').

In complete contrast to the other two, here is a thirty-second commercial in which sound and vision blend in a fast-moving extravaganza. It is meaningless to ask which of the two components is more important than the other. One might draw a parallel with composite art-forms such as ballet, in which music and visual spectacle combine to achieve a certain unity of effect:

VISION	SOUND
Open on BCU smiling face of father.	1½ seconds mute.
Pull back to show young daughter, 5–6 years old, piggy-back, laughing.	1st *Voice Over:* Smiles are broader . . .
Cut to young couple under umbrella, laughing.	2nd *Voice Over:* Mouths fresher . . .
Cut to boy tugging at crust of bread. He's about 10.	1st *Voice Over:* Gums are stronger . . .
Cut to girl, 23–25, smiling.	2nd *Voice Over:* Teeth healthier . . .
Mix to toothbrush, tube, paste being squeezed out.	1st *Voice Over:* With new Gibbs S.R.
Cut to girl brushing teeth.	
Cut to animation – *Super in sync.:* 'NEW ACTIVE TINGLE'.	2nd *Voice Over:* It's that new active tingle you feel
Cut to MCU girl brushing teeth.	as fast-foaming new S.R. spreads swiftly round your mouth . . .
Cut to animation. *Quick super:* 'CLEANING'.	1st *Voice Over:* Cleaning!
Cut to MCU girl with brush, head thrown back.	(musical effect)
Cut to animation. *Quick super:* 'REFRESHING'.	Refreshing!

VISION	SOUND
Cut to angled ice-block with radiating lines.	(musical effect)
Cut to animation: *Quick super:* 'PROTECTING'.	Protecting!
Cut to girl brushing teeth	(musical effect)
Super: 'ALL ROUND PROTECTION FOR TEETH AND GUMS!' Zoom in on mouth BCU.	*2nd Voice Over:* Get all-round protection for teeth *and* gums
Cut to pack shot.	in Gibbs S.R. with the new . . . active . . .
Cut to animation. *Quick super in sync:* 'NEW ACTIVE TINGLE'.	*1st Voice Over:* tingle!
Optical to animation – S.R.	

Notice that the supers in this advertisement, which form part of the general medley of visual impressions, coincide everywhere with identical parts of the commentary; they are visual reinforcements of the important parts of the spoken copy, and without the sound track would not make up a coherent message.

This kind of fantasy sequence is a favourite visual accompaniment for jingles. As the linguistic content of jingles is relatively unimportant, there is even less cause for them to be closely integrated with the visual component. Here is a specimen:

S – M – A – R – T – I – E – S
Wot a lot you get
Wot a lot I got
Wot a lot we got
Wot a lot of fun you get
When you ask for a tube of Smarties.
Smarties, milk chocolate Smarties.
A tube of Smarties means
Lots and lots of chocolate beans.
Yes, you get lots and lots and lots
    and lots of Smarties.

The video of this commercial shows a boy and a girl playing with musical instruments, eating Smarties, and generally having a good time. Both of them are obviously having 'lots of fun' and 'lots of Smarties'; but there is no more specific connection than this between the song and what happens on the screen.

The texts of the S.R. and Smarties commercials, unlike the two earlier commercials, involve no reference to accompanying visual events. This contrast can be more generally applied to a rough distinction, in direct address advertising, between practical and emotive appeals to the consumer. Demonstration advertisements, which aim to persuade by visual 'proof', belong to the former category, whereas fantasy commercials belong to the latter. The 'look at this' type of copy stimulates the viewer to *observe* the visual content; but the purpose of an emotively oriented commercial is better served if our rational and observational faculties remain quiescent.

Nevertheless, most of the standard ingredients of direct address copy override such distinctions of psychological strategy. The Gibbs S.R. commentary contains comparatives (*broader, fresher,* etc.); the imperative *get*; repetitions of the brand-name; parataxis ('Cleaning! Refreshing! Protecting!'); adjectival compounds (*all-round, fast-foaming*). All these are characteristic of direct address advertising generally. Whatever minor internal differences there may be, direct address advertising English is a highly homogenous and specialised variety of English.

Indirect Address Advertising

One way to approach the language of indirect address advertising is to observe the various degrees to which it *lacks* the homogeneity of the language of direct address advertising. That it is on the whole less homogenous follows from the fact that secondary situations themselves vary from one advertisement to another. A secondary participant's speech will vary, for example, according to what kind of person he is meant to be, and what kind of relationship is intended to exist between him and other secondary participants, or the viewer. In a sense, the language of direct address is the language of pure salesmanship and that of indirect address, a diluted version of it.

Monologue. In the television monologue situation the viewer is addressed by a secondary participant who usually appears on the screen, at least for part of the time in which he or she is talking. Monologue speech is closest to direct address commentary when the speaker is a 'presenter', someone who is little more than a visible vehicle for the advertising message:

> *Girl:* Have you seen the Newsome Cloth Test? Look! I paint ink on both these materials, then wash with water. Only the Newsome Cloth comes quite clean. Insist on Newsome Cloth for your next sports jacket.

This is only distinguishable from direct demonstration copy by one trivial feature: the use of the first person pronoun *I*, which indicates that the person delivering the message is actually participating in the demonstration.

The most common type of monologue participant is the testifying consumer, a person who purportedly recommends the product on the basis of personal experience. A testifying consumer, unlike a presenter, needs to be given some identifiable personality and background. But the borderline between the two is not always clear. Here, for instance, is a piece of copy which bears no salient marks of personality, and differs little from what we would expect from the anonymous 'voice over':

> *Young Wife:* Bri-nylon sweaters are marvellous! At last we have high-fashion knitwear that can be washed by hand, and in the washing machine. Bri-nylon dries perfectly, never bobbles or shrinks, and the colour stays bright. There's nothing like Bri-nylon, because all Bri-nylon sweaters are easy to wash – even in a washing machine.

Here as before a pronoun provides the only real clue that this is not direct address language: a pronoun *we* which can only mean 'we consumers'. The script says that the speaker 'is about twenty-three', and 'has been married for about a year to an engineer with good prospects'. But all we gather from her manner of speech is that she talks very like an advertisement! Perhaps it should be added (as there are no imperatives or *you*s) that she talks like an advertisement which is rather subdued in its tone of appeal to the viewer. The last sentence of this commercial is the part which associates it most clearly with direct, rather than indirect address copy. 'There's nothing like x' (where x is the brand-name) is a cliché of 'pure' advertising language; so also is the peculiarity of repeating in a *because* clause a brand-name already mentioned in the main clause: '... Bri-nylon, because Bri-nylon ...'. These are so patently 'advertisingese' that they might seem forced coming from the lips of a secondary participant.

However, the effect at this point is not too unnatural, as the speaker has moved so close to the camera that nothing is seen except the texture of her sweater: she is no longer addressing the public from the screen, and has become effectively a 'voice over'.

This example reveals the potentiality of a conflict between language which is 'natural' to a secondary participant (i.e. is an appropriate way for a private individual to talk), and language which fully incorporates the salesmanlike qualities of direct address copy. The two monologue scripts already quoted aim at selling effectiveness rather than appropriateness to the speaker as a person. But as the greatest strength of the monologue situation lies in the personal appeal and authenticity of the speaker, most monologue copy differs more markedly from direct address copy. The three examples below illustrate the flexibility of monologue language in respect of the individual character and role of the speaker:

Newspaper Compositor: Why do I roll my own? Well – I always roll my own because if I didn't I couldn't smoke Old Holborn. That's why I roll my own. Good Old Holborn.

Corporal: This is a tough exercise all right. We must be near the dropping zone now. Yes, this is it. Here come the helicopters and the paras. Hmm. What a do this is. Tonight we're going up through those woods. We think they're dug in up there. (Pause) They were there all right. We were almost on top of them before they saw us. The Major wasn't half chuffed. One of the best exercises we've been on. Ah, it's good to be back, though – steak and chips never tasted so good, and I've got a month's leave coming up. Plenty of money to enjoy it with too.

Lapcell man's voice (encouraging): Come on mate – match the pattern! (*Aside to viewers*). Taking 'is time – you'd think 'e was using *Lapcell* paste. (*Anxious*) (*Voice Over*) Only *Lapcell* 'll give you all *that* time! You'll never slide it now, mate! Look at that! 'E *was* using Lapcell! *Lapcell* gives you stronger stick – no stain – easier SL–I–I–I–DE! *Lapcell* makes it all so easy.

Incidentally, these scripts illustrate something of the variety of possible uses of a secondary participant. In the first, a standard monologue situation, the compositor is seen on the screen, and addresses the viewer throughout. In the second, the voice is off the screen, commenting on the visible actions of its owner. In the third, the speaker is an animated figure who is sometimes on the screen and sometimes off; he addresses some of his remarks (apparently) to himself, some to the amateur paperhanger who is demonstrating Lapcell paste on the screen, and some to the viewer.

The Old Holborn advertisement shows how monologue can be used to bring the illusion of a personal rapport between speaker and viewer. The following transcription of the opening question represents graphically its intonation contour:

$$\text{Why do } I \text{ roll my }_o w^{n}?$$

(The italicised portion represents a nuclear syllable; see the brief discussion of intonation on p. 21). This is a *Wh-* question with a rising tone, which has the force of a question about a question: 'Did you ask me whether I roll my own?' It is as if the television set were a two-way channel of communication, and the compositor and the viewer were continuing a conversation already started. The role of intonation in direct address advertising is fairly restricted, as many intonation contrasts in English signal personal attitudes and contextual presuppositions which can scarcely apply to one-way public communication. This restriction does not apply to monologue advertising, as it is often part of the purpose of the script to simulate the properties of private colloquy which require varied intonation. Here are the last two sentences of the same script as they were actually spoken.

$$\text{That's } _{why} I \text{ roll my ow}^{n.}$$

$$Go_{o}{}_d \text{ Old } Hol^{born.}$$

The nucleus on *I* and the final rise on *own* indicate a rather diffident attitude: 'Mind you, that's just *my* opinion – I can't vouch for others'. The intonation of 'Good Old Holborn' places it in a class of idiomatic expletives ('Good old Betsy', etc.) expressing affection for a trusted friend. These and other aspects of the speech make it familiar in tone and inclined to masculine understatement – two ways in which it contrasts with normal direct address copy.

The Regular Army commercial is far more slangy and casual than is desirable in direct address. Army slang (*paras* and *chuffed*), together with idiomatic sentences ('What a do this is'; 'I've got a month's leave coming up') bring realism into the part. Much of the script is given over to generating enough human and dramatic interest to involve the viewer, and to painting an attractive picture of army life. Here is another direction in which monologue copy moves away from 'pure' sales language – by devoting itself to a dramatic task which is only obliquely concerned with the advertising message.

The Lapcell advertisement is interesting from the point of view of intonation: it contains three examples of the rise-fall tone, which conveys a certain range of personal attitudes, and does not occur in direct address advertising:

On$_{ly}$ *Lap*^{ce}ll 'll give you all $^{th}_{at}$ ti$^{.me!}$

You'll *ne*^{ve}r slide it ^{no}w, ma$^{te!}$

'E *was* ^{u}sing Lapcell!

(A contour line above each example indicates the position of the rise-fall.) The advantage of a cartoon character is that being himself a violation of realistic conventions, he is not fettered by normal standards of believable behaviour either linguistically or otherwise. Towards the end of this commercial (from 'Lapcell gives you . . .' onwards) the Lapcell man becomes the mouthpiece for orthodox selling language – something which would have been out of character for the compositor and the corporal.

Making the speaker seem alive and credible means not only adapting his remarks to the secondary situation, but giving him language in keeping with his social status, sex, age, and so on. These two desiderata, in the terminology of this book, are respectively REGISTER and DIALECT appropriateness. In monologue, slang and familiar forms of language generally contribute to both, in that they help not only to fix the identity and social background of the speaker, but also to put him on a relaxed, familiar footing with his audience. Factors of phonetic transmission (accent, tone of voice) also play a part. The compositor speaks with a homely London voice; the Lapcell man (for whom anything goes) speaks in an exaggerated cockney; the Regular Army corporal speaks with the kind of voice that army corporals are supposed to have.

Dialogue. The dialogue situation, in which secondary participants address one another, is still further removed from the primary situation than is monologue, and its language has accordingly a still more distant affinity to the language of direct address. The viewer is no longer directly involved in the secondary situation; he has the status of spectator. All the same, dialogue probably has the advantage over monologue in interest appeal: it is said that there is nothing ordinary people enjoy more than watching other ordinary people go about their intimate day-to-day business. The most common type of advertising dialogue on television is a playlet whose dramatis personae are average men, women, or children; whose theme is the excellence of the advertised product, and whose plot is an unremarkable happening of everyday life. This one is a domestic conversation which takes place as the husband is leaving for work:

> *Wife:* Got some nice beef in 'em today, Ted.
> *Husband:* Ta!
> *Wife:* Ooh, nearly forgot your Kit Kat.
> *Husband:* Ooh.
> *Wife:* Stocked up for the week, yesterday.
> *Husband:* That's it. I got to have a Kit Kat with me lunch.

Language in the dialogue situation, even more than in monologue, is determined by considerations of dramatic realism. Serious dramatists can afford to pay little heed to this quality, on the principle that art is not a reproduction of real-life happenings. The copywriter, who has no artistic pretensions of this kind, does not despise the triviality of real-life conversation. In fact by deviating from it he stands to lose credibility and viewer-involvement, which are usually basic ingredients of the effect he wants to achieve. In the Kit Kat commercial he has gone about as far as is practicable in the direction of representing how people actually talk; he even brings in the emphasis on the product in a fairly believable way. So the language of the dialogue is almost as unlike the language of direct advertising as is the language of impromptu colloquial conversation.

A second example of dialogue goes even further in imitating the banality of an everyday language situation:

> *Grocer:* . . . Your daughter was in earlier, she's looking well. There
> you are madam. . . . (pause) . . . anything else?
> *Customer:* No, that's all, thank you. I must just pop along . . .
> (Sound effects: Till ringing) . . . to the butcher's before they close.
> (Sound effects: Till drawer being closed.)
> *Grocer:* Your change madam. Good-day.
> *Customer:* Good-day.

Such commonplace civilities must be exchanged hundreds of times a day in small shops throughout the country. There is no doubt of the realism. What is especially remarkable is the irrelevance of the total dialogue to the primary advertising situation. There are not even any references to the product. The point of the secondary situation has nothing to do with the dialogue, and lies in a mime in which madam at first forgets, then at last remembers, to take the right brand of tea from the shelf.

The advertising value of this dialogue lies, paradoxically, in its apparent lack of connection with advertising; a type of contextual incongruity. If all dialogues were on these lines, they would contribute nothing except interest appeal to the advertisement. There is bound to be some conflict between realism and pertinence to the selling point. Everyone has come across advertisements which overstep the limit in the other direction, by making one fictional consumer zealously declaim the merits of the product to another, who responds with equal zeal. Although such ideal behaviour on the part of a consumer is not unheard of, it is almost as unlikely as a sermon preached in a swimming-bath.

One class of offenders in this field used to be the strip-cartoon press advertisements in which someone's conversion to the product and consequent success in love, work, marriage or life in general, came about through a timely word from a frank friend or professional expert. The timely word would, in fact, be a forthright sales talk in the manner of direct address copy. A recent Lifebuoy advertisement handles this point of the story differently. The frank friend's disclosure fades at the crucial moment: 'Look, don't take this the wrong way, but it *could* be something to do with personal freshness. Why don't you try . . .' Then, into the next panel is inserted a piece of direct address advertising:

> Lifebuoy's deodorant ingredient, Puralin, kills the bacteria which
> cause B.O. Each time you wash, the deodorant protection builds up
> on your skin and guards you against B.O. – day in – day out.

This stratagem avoids the embarrassment of the unrealistic sales talk by a temporary reversion to the primary advertising situation: the situation to which sales talk is appropriate. This is similar to the procedure whereby the conflict between realism and pertinence to the primary situation is usually resolved in television advertising: the dialogue is followed by a short piece of direct address or monologue copy, making explicit what has been implied by example in the secondary situation. The Kit Kat commercial quoted earlier ends with the slogan 'Have a break. Have a Kit Kat', which brings home by direct exhortation the message acted out in the dialogue.

We have seen that the dialogue situation and the primary situation are so different that transposing to one language appropriate to another results in incongruity. Dialogue language and monologue language differ from direct address language in the same direction, but the tendency in dialogue is more extreme. All the same there is a significant amount of common ground between direct address and dialogue copy, for dialogue, in spite of its extraneous 'human interest' component, is at least partly concerned with extolling the virtues of the product. This can easily be illustrated from ordered lists of the most frequent adjectives (from the television sample) in commentary and dialogue:

Commentary: 1. *new*; 2. *good/better/best*; 3. *free*; 4. *fresh*; 5. *delicious*; 6. *full* and *sure*;

Dialogue: 1. *good/better/best*; 2. *sure*; 3. *delicious*; 4. *nice*; 5. *handy, light*, and *little*.

The overlap shows not only in the high position of *good* in both lists (it is in any case one of the most frequent adjectives in English), but in the popularity of the adjectives *sure* and *delicious*, which have obvious applications in salesmanship. Monologue, as might be expected, lies between the two. Of its four most frequent adjectives *good*, *new*, *delicious*, and *nice*, the first three are found in the direct address list, whereas the first, third and fourth are in the dialogue list.

Fiction and non-fiction. The discussion of dialogue and monologue copy has so far been based on quotations from the language of fictional speakers. However, this does not limit the validity of the points made, which, put in a slightly different way, are equally applicable to the language used by 'real' people introduced as secondary participants. Here are some examples of the latter type of copy:

(*a*) Monologue: testimony by an ordinary consumer (the consumer is usually, as in this case, the type of person who might be considered an authority on the kind of product advertised).

John Roach: I'm a great, great, great nephew of old Uncle Tom Cobley, for four generations my family has been born and bred on this farm, and I've got four children to carry on after me. I like a nice bit of cheddar cheese if it's real cheddar and fresh. That's why I like Crackerbarrel by Kraft. It is kept fresh by the special wrapping, and it is a natural cheese.

(*b*) Monologue: testimony by a celebrity.

Danny Blanchflower: Hello there! Yes it's me Danny Blanchflower – meet my family. We all kick off with Shredded Wheat and hot milk for breakfast. (Effects: football match excitement.) Shredded Wheat gives us energy – something I need in my job. (Effects: subtle change from football match noise to that of children's playground.) And my kids – like yours – use up energy all day. (Effects: mattress being turned.) So does my wife – well, *you* know what it's like running a home.

(*c*) Dialogue: interview of an ordinary consumer.

Interviewer: Well Miss Speedie, you do a very unusual job. I bet nobody could guess what your line of business is?

Miss Speedie: I'm a company director and secretary. Since my father and Mr. Scott died a few years ago, I have been carrying on with another director – oh don't misunderstand me – (laughs).

Interviewer: What sort of job is it?

Miss Speedie: Building and contracting. We build factories, churches, schools, and houses of course.

Interviewer: Busy day?

Miss Speedie: Yes, we start at nine in the morning till about six in the evening, and I can assure you I drink more Lucozade in the office than I do at home.

Interviewer: Well, Miss Speedie, I'm not a doctor, but can you tell me in simple language what do you feel Lucozade does for you?

Miss Speedie: Well, just exactly what it says on the label on the bottle.

(*d*) Dialogue: interview of an employee of the advertiser.

Interviewer: This is Doug Jagger – he's a toffee sampler at Mackintosh's. Now, what's the secret of Mackintosh's Toff-O-Luxe, Doug?

Doug Jagger: It's the quality of flavour which makes Mackintosh's Toff-O-Luxe so special.

Interviewer: How do you control that?

Doug Jagger: I take a sample from three hundred toffee boilings every day for testing by our research people.

Interviewer: To make sure it's all of the same high standard, eh?

Doug Jagger: That's right – and that's one reason why Mackintosh's Toff-O-Luxe is always so delicious.

Credibility is a dominant consideration in both fictional and non-fictional indirect address, although its implications are slightly different. For a fictional participant, it is the result of making an actor play the part of a real person convincingly. For a non-fictional participant, it is the result of making a real person play the part of *himself* as convincingly as if he were a professional actor. By employing a celebrity who is also an experienced broadcaster, the advertising agency may find the ideal solution to this problem, and also gain the association of the celebrity's prestige. With the 'man in the street', there are two opposite perils: that he will be so *unlike* himself as to deliver the message in a forced, mechanical way; and that he will be so *like* himself as to display the diffidence and incoherence that is characteristic of real-life behaviour. In practice, the aim is to achieve a happy medium between these two. So from this rather paradoxical analysis we reach the conclusion that the language of non-fictional secondary participants closely resembles that of fictional ones: it is a type of language which compromises between absolute realism and advertising impact.

One difference, however, lies in the fact that practically all non-fiction dialogues are interviews. As the interview is merely a means of eliciting a testimony, non-fiction dialogue tends to be linguistically much closer to monologue than is its fictional counterpart.

Other kinds of indirect address advertising. Monologue and dialogue are the most important, but not the only indirect address situations. Recalling the way in which such situations were defined according to their first and second person participants, we can see that there are these two further possibilities: (*a*) language addressed by the advertiser to a secondary participant; (*b*) language addressed by a secondary participant to the advertiser. Both of them might at first glance seem improbable, but they occasionally occur. The latter situation (secondary participant to advertiser) is that of the testimonial letter ('Mrs. B. of Northampton writes . . .') still widely used in direct mail advertising. The former (advertiser to secondary participant) may occur in television advertising

in the form of an apostrophe from the 'voice over' to a fictional participant. The following commercial shows 'Joe', the paper boy, eating a
hurried breakfast of Corn Flakes before he begins his rounds. The sung
part of the commentary refers to him in the third person, whereas the
concluding spoken part addresses him in the second person:

> (Sung):   A paper boy's life's an early one
>   But Joe can help himself to sun
>   Before he starts his paper run
>   He always eats his Corn Flakes.

> (Spoken): There's nothing like Kellogg's Corn Flakes to cheer you
> up in the morning. Never mind if people are a bit stand-offish. And
> don't worry about the time – you've got the sun on your side.

This example reminds us that the copywriter can exercise theatrical licence
in using apostrophes (remarks addressed to someone or something unable
to hear them or answer back) and asides (remarks heard by the audience,
but not by other secondary participants). Another dramatic device of this
kind is soliloquy, which has a well-known manifestation in the balloons
headed 'THINKS . . .' in strip-cartoons. It is used more subtly in television
copy such as the following, which purports to represent the 'audible
thoughts' of a housewife in a supermarket:

> Ooh Crackerbarrel – new shape . . . new foil wrapping too . . .
> should keep the cheese nice and fresh. As there's no rind – no waste.
> Such a good natural cheddar . . . and there's a choice of two flavours.
> I'll take both.

This interior monologues technique does not so much confront the viewer
with the personality of a secondary participant, as invite her to *identify*
herself with a secondary participant, and see the product through her
eyes. She is approached by suggestion rather than overt persuasion.
Linguistically, this is in some ways the type of indirect address copy
which approaches most closely to that of direct address. Compare the
following piece of body copy from a women's journal:

> The taste of **real** coffee. Rich. Smooth. Mellow. The taste of Camp.
> Made **with** good coffee, made as good coffee should be. Fresh
> ground. Gently percolated. Then concentrated, not into a dehy-
> drated powder, but into a full-flavoured **liquid**. With chicory to
> give it 'bite'. And sweetened with pure cane sugar. Coffee at its best.

Ready for you to enjoy. And you can enjoy **forty-two cups** of marvellous Camp coffee **for only 2/7½d.**★

This is direct address language: we can see this from the use of *you* (= 'you readers') instead of *I*. But its disjunctive grammatical structure suggests a stream of half-formed thoughts rather than a connected line of argument. We might say that it is imitating the technique of an interior monologue. This impressionistic style of approach is not unusual in modern direct address copy.

★ The exact typography of press advertisements will be reproduced only when it serves an illustrative purpose. Typographical emphasis *within body copy* will be indicated by bold type, as in this example, whether capitals, italics, bold type, or underlining were used in the original.

Chapter 6

Products, Media, Audiences, Aims

Products, media, audiences, aims – these four words, which played a part in the general definition of the primary advertising situation, are now to be made the basis for a limited discussion of different *types* of advertising, and their relevance to the study of advertising language. Instead of being content with such broad generalisations as 'the consumer' and 'the product', we shall ask questions like 'For what kind of consumer?' and 'For what kind of product?' Linguistic differences depending on such factors are subtle and difficult to analyse, so I shall attempt to cover only a few topics of interest and significance.

Products

Advertising different kinds of product obviously means making different choices of language, and in particular different choices of vocabulary. The trouble is that such differences are often obvious and trivial. We do not need to be told that advertisements for cars will frequently contain such items as *car*, *engine*, *brakes*, and *drive*. This follows from the general truth that advertisements talk about the products they advertise. If vocabulary items are classified by the word classes in which they function, the study of noun vocabulary is particularly unrewarding. This is because the majority of nouns in consumer advertising copy are concrete, and refer directly to the product, to features and parts of the product, or to people and objects connected with it.

Adjective vocabulary, on the other hand, can be highly informative. In a recent study of press advertising,* E. O. O. Winter selected for comparison batches of newspaper advertisements for two classes of product, patent medicine and women's clothing. The study showed that copy for each product group had a remarkably homogeneous vocabulary, reflecting in part the general homogeneity of adjective vocabulary in advertising, and in part the advertising habits and strategies associated with

---

* *The Language of Contemporary Newspaper Advertisements in English*, University of London M.A. thesis (April, 1964).

the class of product. The most favoured adjectives (in order) in women's clothing advertising were the following:

1. *new*	5. *free*	9. *easy*	13. *smooth*	17. *fashionable*
2. *good*	6. *full*	10. *light*	14. *luxurious*	18. *practical*
3. *soft*	7. *lovely*	11. *high*	15. *slim*	19. *washable*
4. *warm*	8. *wonderful*	12. *perfect*	16. *smart*	

Certain items in this list (*soft*, *warm*, *smart*, *practical*, *washable*) indicate desirable qualities particularly associated with the product group; some of these have a vague imaginative appeal, whereas others (e.g. *washable*) designate more utilitarian virtues. Other adjectives, including the first two items on the list, *new* and *good*, are part of the general stock vocabulary of advertising, and have no special relevance to the product group.

Beyond vocabulary, linguistic variations according to the product advertised are not particularly conspicuous. But at least one of the striking differences between Winter's two samples of advertising material lay in the area of grammar. This was a large disparity in the frequency of 'minor sentences', or sentences not containing a main predicator. Minor sentences are associated with media of elementary communication, such as titles, labels, road-signs, and posters. The reason for this contrast is not hard to find. Patent medicine copy is typically of the type which aims to win the consumer by explanations of how the product works and what benefits it brings. Consequently it tends to contain long unbroken stretches of discursive prose. Women's clothing advertisements, on the other hand, characteristically have short pieces of body copy, and emphasise by illustrations, headlines, and captions the imaginative appeal of the product. In addition, the body copy is often used to describe in a rather impressionistic manner the qualities of the product; it is emotionally descriptive, rather than explanatory. Both these factors favour a 'primitive' (or, in the terminology of this book, disjunctive) kind of grammar in which minor sentences are abundant.

Media

Press, television, posters, films, direct mail: these are among the media which may be chosen, for one reason or another, as the best means of reaching the public. What I have to say concerns only press and television, and involves the most basic contrast of medium – that of spoken versus written communication.

To understand differences in language between press and television advertisements, we have to appreciate some essential differences in their design and structure. The standard components of press advertisements, as distinguished by function and lay-out, are:

Headline
[*Illustration(s)*]
Body copy: The main part of the advertising message, often divided into various sections under *subheads.*
Signature line: A mention of the brand-name, often accompanied by a price-tag, slogan, trade-mark, or picture of the brand pack.
Standing details: Cut-out coupons, and strictly utilitarian information in small print, usually appearing unchanged on a series of different advertisements – the address of the firm; how to obtain further information; legal footnotes; etc.

The preferred order of these sections is (from top to bottom) as listed, and there is also a priority of inclusion: the headline and signature line can be regarded as the most indispensable parts of a press advertisement, although even these are sometimes collapsed into a single display line. The other parts are definitely optional, and are omitted with varying degrees of frequency.

This scheme is an idealisation, for there is clearly a great deal of latitude in the way an advertisement may be constructed and set out. As a press advertisement is two-dimensional, the notion of order demands a certain freedom of interpretation. An illustration might occupy the whole length of the advertisement, and the various linguistic components be placed at different positions to the right or left of it; or the headline or other parts of the verbal message might be superimposed on the illustration. Besides, any concept of uniform design has to be weighed against the unpredictable and capricious element in advertising. It is the practitioner's prerogative to break with the conventions of his profession wherever he feels the special advantages outweigh the penalties. So, for example, it is even possible to find press advertisements (called 'headless wonders' by David Ogilvy*) which lack headlines; and press advertisements which have no brand signature (concealing the brand identification in the body copy).

The various copy sections of an advertisement have different functions, and therefore different linguistic characteristics, which will emerge from time to time in later chapters.

---

* Ogilvy (1964), p. 130.

The scheme I have presented for press advertisements is easily modified to suit other types of visual advertising. Posters, for example, have the same outline structure; the difference lies in a more frequent omission of body copy and standing details.

Do television commercials have any kind of equivalent for each of the copy sections noted above? There is only one clean division to be made in television language on grounds of physical transmission: that between copy to be spoken (commentary) and copy to be written (supers). This really makes a threefold classification, as there is a choice between simultaneous aural and visual transmission, and each independently. All can be seen in the following seven-second commercial. In the transcription, italicised portions are 'supered' and capitalised portions are in the spoken commentary (so italicised capitals represent simultaneous sound and vision):

Trebor. REAL FRUIT CENTRES. SOFT CENTRES. *TREBOR BITTER ORANGE, 3d. TREBOR* BITTER LEMON. *3d.*

None of these categories really corresponds to any category of press copy. In vision alone, we commonly find titles which form an introduction to each of a series of commercials: 'Chivers casebook'; 'Life with Katie'; 'Around the house with Addis'. These are not to be equated with headlines; their press equivalent is a rarity. Also routine information roughly corresponding to the standing details of press copy is often conveyed by supers alone; for example, price information, and the manufacturer's identification, when this is not included in the name of the product: 'A product of Nabisco Foods Limited'; 'Made by Kia-Ora'. Supers synchronised with the spoken commentary are largely brand-names and key phrases containing the main selling proposition: 'Oats and wheat' (for a breakfast cereal); 'In four width fittings' (for children's shoes); 'Specially made for Town living' (for a shampoo). There seems to be a definite similarity between this component of a television commercial and the signature line of press copy. But it is a more important element of television copy, and may include repetitions throughout the advertisement.

Also, the proportions of television copy I have compared with the signature line may be incorporated in the spoken commentary without vision. In the following commercial, these key portions are in italics; like the rest of the commentary, they are unaccompanied by supers:

This is the tip, this is the blend, this is the smoke that's setting the trend. *Bachelor!* The trend is to tipped, and the tip is Bachelor.

Because Bachelor's the tip that gives real tobacco taste. *Bachelor.*
Britain's most smoked tipped cigarette. This is the tip, this is the blend,
this is the smoke that's setting the trend. *Player's Bachelor.*

The majority of commercials have what can be called an 'endline', containing the signature line feature we have just been examining. The
endline may be simply a final mention of the brand-name, as in the
example above; or it may include price or a slogan. It is often synchronised
with supers, and is often combined with an equally standardised part of
the visual sequence: the concluding pack shot. Some typical endlines are:
'Sparkling Tango'; 'Feel the difference with Bristow's Lanolin Shampoo';
'Carnival – the fabulous fully-fashioned stockings by Morley'; 'Matinee
tipped – a fine Virginia cigarette. 3/2 for 20.'

The most marked difference between the two media as regards copy
and design is the lack of any television equivalent to the headline. At the
beginning of a commercial, which is the obvious place to look for such a
correspondence, we are very often plunged without introduction into a
monologue or dialogue situation. A direct address opening partly
corresponds in function to a headline, in that it aims at capturing the interest of the viewer, and at the same time steering it towards the main
selling point. Favourite openings are questions ('Running a tempera-
ture?'), *when* clauses ('When there's a baby in the house. . . .'), and *if*
clauses ('If you suffer from indigestion . . .'). But of course television has
nothing corresponding to the typographical separation of headline and
body copy. There is also a difference of purpose, which David Ogilvy
expresses as follows: 'When you advertise in magazines and newspapers,
you must start by attracting the reader's attention. But in television the
viewer is already attending; your problem is not to frighten her away'.[*]

Television also, of course, has no equivalent of the subhead. There is an
interesting linguistic consequence of this and of the lack of a television
equivalent to the headline. In press copy, one type of minor sentence is
more or less restricted to headlines and subheads. It is the type which con-
consists of an embedded *wh-* clause: 'Why Spry makes the lightest
pastry'; 'How to relieve tense nervous headaches'. Although quite
common in the press, this construction scarcely occurs at all in television
copy.

Our structural comparison of press and television advertisements has
given grounds for expecting considerable differences in language apart

---

[*] Ogilvy (1964), p. 161.

from those regularly associable with the distinction between spoken and written English (see pp. 85–90). But in fact it is the similarity, rather than the contrast, between television and press copy that needs explanation. One tentative explanation is that as the same people are involved in the writing of press and television copy, they tend to carry over to one medium the techniques applicable to the other. For example, some aspects of the disjunctive syntax of television commentary (see pp. 95–6) might be attributable to an unmotivated transfer to the newer medium of habits associated with headlines and signatures lines in print. Likewise there may be grounds for supposing that the opposite has recently been taking place: that a style of copy in television advertising is having some effect on the composition of press copy. Here is the copy of a 1964 press advertisement:

> **Enjoy that famous Player's taste.** When you smoke a Player's and enjoy that famous Player's taste, always so fresh and inviting, then you know why of all cigarettes only Player's please so much.
> **Only Player's please so much.**

The restrained use of display suggests a surrender of the attention-compelling advantages of print in favour of the purely sequential use of language, as in television commentary. The amount of repetition is highly characteristic of television advertising; also, the final sentence, which simply repeats the last five words of the body copy, acts more like a television endline than a press signature line. Here is another piece of press copy which is extremely repetitious; it contains ten occurrences of the lexical item *soft*, including those in the brand-name:

Headline: the super-soft toilet tissue
Izal Soft
the only toilet tissue that's softened with LANOLIN

Body copy: Izal Soft – so soft and gentle, because it's the only toilet tissue that's softened with lanolin. And only lanolin gives you and your whole family that very special soothing softness . . . that Izal **super** softness. They'll welcome the gentleness of this softest toilet tissue. Next time you shop choose Izal Soft in any of five fresh colours.

However, there is a less speculative and more important reason for the similarity of press and television copy: the advertising world's assumption that highly readable copy means copy which is also easy to read out and listen to. Copywriters read their work aloud to test its effectiveness, even though it may be destined for print. So whatever *involuntary* transfer there may be, there is certainly an *intentional* transfer of the spoken mode to the written mode. Press copy, like television copy, tends to follow a co-ordinative pattern, whereby one structure is added to another in a simple concatenated sequence, rather than the more intricate pattern of periodic sentence structure, classically associated with written English. This is apparent in the punctuation of press copy, which is peculiar largely because it imitates the rhythms of speech and expounds a kind of grammatical patterning far removed from that which punctuation normally has to deal with.

Audiences

Some variations in advertising language can be attributed to the nature of the envisaged audience: for example, how it is limited as regards age, sex, social status, or geographical area.

Some specialised types of advertising, such as are found in trade, business, and industrial journals, are addressed to members of particular occupational classes. Another restricted type of public is reached through magazines catering for leisure interests: motoring, sport, music and so on. Advertising copy for such selective readerships tends to follow the 'reason-why' approach, and often includes technical terms not widely understood outside its audience.

An advertisement's 'audience' can mean either the public it is intended to reach, or the public it actually reaches – for instance, the total reader-ship of the publication in which it appears. How to correlate these two is the headache of the advertising media expert: I shall not need to dis-tinguish between them. On television, perhaps the least selective of media, the intended audience is sometimes summoned by a vocative, as in these two introductory appeals:

Men – see the wonderful Morley County Sweaters – in pure Botany wool.

Hey fellahs! girls! They're *giving* away games!

This is about the only use of the vocative in direct address advertising.

The importance of selecting language appropriate to a particular category of consumer can be overemphasised. Often no attempt is made to adapt the advertising approach or advertising language to different audiences; identical advertisements appear in popular and 'quality' publications, in publications of different regional circulations, and in publications of specialised and general interest.

Differences of language are most noticeable in advertising addressed to audiences differing in social or educational standing. One kind of difference is a larger admixture of unorthodox copy in 'quality' publications. This seems to stem from the feeling that highbrows are relatively unmoved by standard sales talk, and have to be wooed through advertising which has an intellectual or 'off-beat' appeal. All the same, there is a style of copy which could be described as 'typical' for this type of public:

> There's more than sun drenched beaches and delightful hotels in Malta. Set in the heart of the Mediterranean, Malta has a unique fascination, all of its own. You can go swimming, skin-diving, water ski-ing, deep-sea fishing; or you can explore Neolithic ruins, Catacombs, the Roman Villa or admire the magnificent grandeur of the palaces and cathedral of the Knights of St. John of Jerusalem. And Malta's only 4½ hours from London by air.

This body copy section of an advertisement in the *Sunday Times Supplement* is adapted to its audience in several respects – in its use of the abstract nouns *fascination* and *grandeur*; of recondite words such as *Neolithic* and *catacombs*. Its vocabulary is less familiar and its syntax less simple than that which typifies advertising in popular publications. But stress should also be laid on its similarity to popular advertising copy. It contains such typically colloquial features as the reduced form of *is* after *there* (*there's*) and even after a noun (*Malta's*). It contains the advertising cliché 'You can . . .', and the inevitable list of advantages: 'swimming, skin-diving, water ski-ing, deep-sea fishing'. It is standard advertising English with a difference.

Aims

As the intention of the message is ultimately the defining criterion of advertising, distinctions of aim *within* advertising can be no more than matters of emphasis. Most of this book is concerned with advertising which promotes a product, and up to now I have left out of the picture advertising which promotes services (banking, insurance, etc.), and advertising which promotes a commercial enterprise: so-called 'prestige' advertising.

Whereas in consumer advertising a firm advertises what it makes, in prestige advertising it advertises itself. The aim is to inspire not action, but good will (amongst shareholders, employees, or the influential public generally). The accent is on the informative aspect of advertising: reporting the firm's achievements. The tone is less urgent than in consumer advertising; imperatives are infrequent, and the more brazen forms of eulogy are absent. Average prestige copy is especially complex, not only because it is directed at an educated and well-informed public, but because it has an involved story to tell. Sometimes a fairly personal and informal mode of expression is preferred (using, for example, *we* in reference to the advertiser and *you* in address to the public). Elsewhere the copywriter adopts a style of objective reporting, as in the following piece from a *Times* special supplement:

> Founded in 1955 on a capital of only £E500,000 – and now the MISR Foreign Trade Company is the most important trading organisation in the UAR, with financial reserves of over £E2,000,000. Nine years of unprecedented success – and today's import and export figures for the UAR are solid proof of this. International markets have been penetrated, vital trade relationships consolidated; while constant research into world marketing conditions has kept the MISR Foreign Trade Company abreast of all important trends and recent developments. Close connections are maintained with leading international factories, and the MISR Foreign Trade Company acts as agent for many foreign manufacturers and commercial houses. An office of the Company is now open in London's West End, and many more are scheduled to open in the near future in important world trading centres. Continual growth and expansion are helping the Company to play an even-larger part in the field of international trade.

One gauge of the aim and intended audience of advertising copy is the range of commendatory items it contains. In the Malta advertisement we find *delightful, magnificent, fascination,* which contrast with their most favoured equivalents in popular advertising: *good, lovely, wonderful,* etc. In prestige advertising, self-eulogy is often hidden in board-room clichés which imply the dynamism, success, and health of the firm's activities. The above example contains 'unprecedented success', 'constant research', 'solid proof', 'continual growth' – phrases in which the adjective is not eulogistic in itself, but has that connotation in conjunction with the following abstract noun.

5—E.I.A.

But there are still some family resemblances between consumer and prestige copy. The quotation contains an example of the familiar superlative construction: 'the most important trading organisation in the UAR'. It also exemplifies disjunctive features which would not be tolerated in more formal types of written English: the first two sentences begin with respectively an independent non-finite clause ('Founded in 1955 on a capital of only £E500,000') and an independent minor clause ('Nine years of unprecedented success'), both co-ordinated with a following finite clause.

Chapter 7

Register

Up to this point I have discussed the advertising situation as a whole, and some of the variable features of this situation which influence the copywriter's choice of language. This has given me a chance to illustrate some of the varied types of language employed in advertising, and incidentally, to show how difficult it can be to generalise about them. Generalisations can, however, be made, and it is the main purpose of this book to make them. We can only arrive at them by broadening our perspective, and looking at English in advertising against the background of other varieties of usage, all functioning within that broadest of generalisations: 'the English language'.

The English language is, in fact, a generalisation of many kinds of linguistic behaviour. Some people are inclined to think of it differently: as an invariant, God-given code of rules. A failure to conform to this code is then explained as a linguistic lapse or aberration. Copywriters, in particular, have often been accused of vitiating or misusing 'the Queen's English'. But as long as we are interested in language description, not language legislation, we cannot take this point of view. People's moral feelings about language are not to be confused with the facts of its use. So we study the copywriter's language in relation to the English language as a whole, not to see where it falls short of 'correct English', but to discover where it resembles and differs from varieties of English used in other contexts. To describe the English of advertising is to say what is distinctive about it: that is, how it differs from other 'Englishes'. If more of this chapter is devoted to those other 'Englishes' than to the English of advertising, my justification is that the latter can only be studied by means of external comparisons.*

'Englishes' or 'varieties of English': such manners of speaking require explanation. Dialectal divisions within a language are familiar. Broadly interpreted, DIALECT refers to any type of English defined as belonging to a particular grouping of speakers. Usually the grouping is made on the

---

* Introductory discussions of diversity in the English language and the status of 'Standard English' are found in Quirk (1962), Chapters 1, 2, 5, and 6.

basis of geographical area, although one may also speak of dialects of sex, age-group, or social class. A brief consideration of regional and national differences is enough to dispose of the myth of the English language as a total, invariant system of rules. Even if it were possible to regard 'Standard English' as a linguistic norm for the whole of the British Isles, there is no doubt of the differences which separate our 'English' from the 'Englishes' of North America, Australasia, or Africa. Differences of accent (that is, of phonology) are the most striking; but there are also differences of grammar and vocabulary: American *checkers, apartment, figure out* contrast with British *draughts, flat, work out*. At the furthest extreme are 'Pidgin Englishes': varieties so unlike any other that it may seem more practical to treat them as foreign languages. Again, however much standardisers and purists may insist that the people who speak these dialects ought to speak like us, the fact is that they do not.

This study is concerned with English according to *use* rather than to *user*. Varieties of English distinguished by use in relation to social context are called REGISTERS.* Whereas dialect differences have long been a subject for scholarly research, register differences have largely remained in the hands of amateur commentators and dogmatisers, and have been acknowledged only in a somewhat haphazard way by grammarians and lexicographers. Along with such abbreviations as *dial.* and *Amer.* in our standard dictionaries, are found *colloq., fam., poet., sl.,* and other indicators of the contextual range to which a word is appropriate. But such stage-directions are generally used sparingly, and are only the very beginning of an analysis of register restrictions in English vocabulary. One register contrast, that between formal and colloquial English, affects a large proportion of our vocabulary, and an even greater proportion of our stock of idioms. *Get, nice, daft, put up with, set-up*: such colloquial words and phrases do not pass muster in formal usage. But neither, for that matter, are *amelioration, unauthorised, decease, alight,* and *medical practitioner* the regular coin of ordinary conversation; if they are used in informal contexts, it is generally with an air of facetious and self-conscious pedantry – that is, with an awareness that they are being used 'out of context'. Large numbers of words are limited to very specialised fields of technical or scientific communication: most of these are omitted by even the more

---

* Discussions of register and the contextual study of language are found in Halliday, McIntosh and Strevens (1964), Chapter 4; and Dixon (1964). In what follows in this chapter, I have also drawn on a draft of a paper by J. O. Ellis, 'On Contextual Meaning', to be published in *In Memory of J. R. Firth*, ed. C. E. Bazell et al. (London, 1966).

voluminous dictionaries. Nor does a lexicographer in the normal way attempt to record the obscure and often short-lived vocabularies of slangs and jargons. They only reach his notice when they begin to pass into general colloquial usage.

Grammatical differences of register are in general not so remarkable as lexical differences. But there are some obvious divergences, and many less obvious ones, between the grammars of (for example) formal and colloquial English. Among the obvious differences is the colloquial use of verbal and negative contractions (*I'll*, *don't*, etc.) instead of the full forms *I will*, *do not*, etc. The domain of register also, to some extent, has its grammatical analogues of Pidgin English: the abbreviated grammar of headlines and telegrams, and the even odder grammars of quasi-symbolic Englishes, such as are used in technical manuals, knitting patterns, and chess game reports.

In Chapters 8, 9, and 10 I shall be plotting some of the major register distinctions in English; or, figuratively speaking, drawing a 'sketch-map' which shows the position of advertising English in relation to other registers. Like any map, it will show only selected features: those that are relevant to its purpose. Most maps (including dialect maps) are two-dimensional objects; but in charting register distinctions, we are concerned with many dimensions. These dimensions will be studied under the three following headings.

Relation between participants. The sort of questions to be asked about participants are: How many people are participating in the act of communication at either end? Are they known to one another well? a little? not at all? Is there any significant difference of social status between them? Register differences chiefly governed by such considerations can be called differences of STYLE OF DISCOURSE (e.g. 'colloquial style'; 'impersonal style'; 'casual style').

Medium. How is the message transmitted from source to audience? Is it spoken or written? broadcast? printed? written to be spoken (scripted)? Register variations chiefly determined by factors of transmission (including circumstances attendant on transmission, such as the degree of feed-back from second person to first person) can be called variations of MODE.

Social function. What part does the linguistic message play as a form of social activity? Different answers to this question will yield varieties of English defined by ROLE. Private roles include greeting, condolence, 'being sociable', giving orders. Among public roles are literature, journalism, legal and scientific writing.* Advertising itself is one of the public roles of language.

Before proceeding to particular dimensions of style of discourse and mode, let us examine some of the principles on which register analysis is based.

Register distinctions are mostly relative, not absolute. Local dialects are often spoken of as if they had well-demarcated geographical limits: the 'Yorkshire dialect', the 'Scottish dialect', the 'London dialect', and so on. Needless to say, dialect maps constructed by observation and research show no such rigid frontiers, except where natural geographical boundaries (sea, mountains, etc.) are real barriers to communication. Different features held to typify one dialect will rarely be located in coextensive areas, and in place of frontiers, there will be overlaps and gradations. In the same way, a register classification does not mean an array of neatly partitioned pigeon-holes. The formal-colloquial contrast, for instance, is best conceived of as a scale on which many positions between two extremes ('most colloquial' and 'most formal') are possible. Distinctions of role are more clear-cut, but even here edges are blurred, as was shown in the discussion of the scope of the word 'advertising' (Chapter 3). In most cases, it is strictly inappropriate to speak of 'dialects' and 'registers' in the plural, or of this, that and the other 'register' in the specific singular. But if a dialectologist shunned expressions of the type 'the dialect of . . .', he would find himself obliged to use uncomfortable periphrases. On a similar plea, I shall feel free to write 'the register of . . .', bearing in mind that it is a convenient abbreviation for 'the range of register variation operating in . . .'

People are often unaware of the register distinctions with which they operate. Any native speaker of English knows, in the sense that he operates with, distinctions of register. As is the case with general language acquisition, he learns most of them without conscious effort: by example, habit, and exercise of the social instinct to conform. In some cases, it is true, explicit tuition plays a part. One of the accomplishments acquired in English lessons at school is a receptive and productive familiarity with the formal

---

* Some of the more interesting public roles of English are exemplified in Quirk (1962), Chapter 10, and in Warburg (1962).

register of the language: the register appropriate to serious, precise communication. To this end, the teacher who follows traditional methods
inculcates rules which inhibit some colloquial forms of expression: 'Never
use *get, nice, don't,* etc. in essays or business letters.' Similar methods may
also be employed in teaching journalistic, scientific, and technical
writing: students are often told about manners of expression which they
ought to avoid. Such rules of thumb are not always negative; they
may recommend, as well as discourage, certain aspects of linguistic
performance.

> Prefer the familiar word to the unfamiliar
> Prefer the concrete word to the abstract
> Prefer the simple word to the complex
> Prefer the short word to the long.

These instructions come from a manual of copywriting,* and are obviously designed to instil a readable style of composition: one that has the
virtue of being easily assimilated and understood by any audience
representative of the 'general public'.

But the consciously learnt aspects of register are rather like the visible
part of an iceberg: they happen to be brought to one's attention, but they
are only a small fraction of the total linguistic performance. This is especially true of advertising. Textbooks of copywriting and general advertising
method give only an occasional linguistic tip; they are understandably far
more concerned with psychological aims and techniques than with the
linguistic means by which these are achieved and carried out. If copywriters use the same linguistic formulae over and over again, it is not
because they have been taught to use them, but because the habit of using
them has been acquired by imitation, and reinforced by experience and
success.

The conventions of register are not inviolable. I have already suggested that
there is no universal, invariant system of rules which can be identified as
'the English language'. It is better to think in terms of two sets of rules:
those 'general' rules which apply to English irrespective of the circumstances in which it is spoken; and those rules of dialect and register which
restrict linguistic behaviour according to user and use. In the case of
register, 'convention' is a more appropriate term than 'rule': the penalty
for breaking a register restriction is rarely so drastic as that of breaking one

---

* De Voe (1956), p. 649.

of the 'general' rules on which we depend for making ourselves intelligible at all.

The effect of ignoring a convention of style of discourse can be equated with that produced by a breach of social etiquette. A formal letter ending 'Thanks a lot, yours faithfully' will probably inspire amusement. Someone who addresses a very close friend: 'Good afternoon, Miss Smith' may well, by that very utterance, terminate the intimacy. In this respect, register is itself a code of social behaviour, capable of influencing other kinds of social behaviour, as well as being influenced by them.

The inhibiting power of conventions of role varies a great deal. The maximum degree of stringency applies to language used in religious and legal rites (for example, oath-taking). Here any divergence from the prescribed form of words annuls the form of social activity concerned. At the other extreme I would place literature: here (at least in modern times) virtually all conventions observed are those which the writer imposes of his own free-will. This is to say that the literary writer (particularly the poet) has in principle the freedom to borrow features from any register of the language for artistic purposes. This freedom is also exercised, to some extent, in ordinary conversation for various comic or sarcastic effects. Advertising, too, must be placed among those roles in which a great versatility of linguistic performance is acceptable. The copywriter is never encumbered by the conventions of copywriting: he breaks them when it suits his purpose. In fact atypical forms of language may have a positive advantage over more conventional copy, in that they are more likely to compel the consumer's attention and interest.

Differences of register are statistically measurable. We turn now to the practical business of observation and analysis. In terms of quantification, 'feature A is appropriate to situation B' means 'feature A has a high probability of occurrence in situation B'. This statement in turn can only be checked by taking a corpus of linguistic material representative of situation B, and counting the number of occurrences of feature A. But even this is only a part of the task: 'frequent' is a relative term, meaning 'more frequent than in other situations'. So to complete the empirical justification of any statement about register, we have to undertake comparisons with similar corpuses drawn from other social contexts.

Fortunately, appeal can be made to another more accessible kind of evidence, the native speaker's experience and operational knowledge of register. This, combined with a detailed (not necessarily statistical) study of relevant texts is sufficient authority for most of the important statements one would want to make about register.

The relation between statistical knowledge and operational knowledge of register is a delicate one. As I explained in the general introduction, the role of frequency analysis, in the present study, is confirmatory rather than fundamental. This is not just a decision of convenience, but an expression of what actually happens: counting occurrences, in a large number of cases, is merely a laborious way of coming to conclusions one has already arrived at subjectively. More detailed quantitative analyses (requiring large corpuses and the aid of computers) can be expected to produce results beyond the insight of the native speaker. But it would be foolish to suggest that no general statements about register can be made until a full statistical analysis of the major registers of English has been carried out. The following register classification rests largely on my own perceptions as to facts of usage; those who perceive differently are at liberty to disagree.

There is also room for disagreement on another matter: not on the facts themselves, but on the way they are categorised. For example, I have chosen to treat style of discourse in terms of bi-polar oppositions: 'colloquial-formal', 'casual-ceremonial', etc. Others may feel that some of these oppositions are better treated as belonging to a single dimension of contrast.* However this may be, the aims of the classification are simplicity and suitability to the present task of relating advertising English to other registers of the language.

---

* Joos (1962) uses a five-point scale of style 'frozen-formal-consultative-casual-intimate'.

Chapter 8

Style of Discourse

The four sets of polarities of style I shall consider under this heading are COLLOQUIAL-FORMAL, CASUAL-CEREMONIAL, PERSONAL-IMPERSONAL and SIMPLE-COMPLEX. Advertising English can be placed on two of these dimensions as 'colloquial' rather than 'formal' and 'simple' rather than 'complex'. Its position relative to the other two cannot be stated so simply. Register dimensions are not necessarily independent of one another: I have just illustrated this point by saying what correlations exist between one variety of English identified by *role* (advertising) and two dimensions of *style*. Similarly, the dimensions of style listed are to some extent mutually determined: 'formal' excludes 'casual'; 'colloquial' tends to imply 'personal' and 'formal' 'impersonal'. Nevertheless there is enough independent variation to warrant their separation.

Colloquial-formal

The circumstances which effect choice of style on this dimension cannot be disposed of in a single sentence. But as a starting point, we may say that the colloquial style is associated with *private* and the formal style with *public* discourse, defining these terms by the number of people involved at the originating and receiving ends of the message. At the receiving end, audiences may vary from nil (in soliloquy) to millions (in a television programme). Is it possible to envisage a similar scale in operation at the source of the message? Certainly not if 'originator' is equated with 'performer': outside comic opera, people do not generally speak in chorus. But as I indicated on pp. 33-4, the distinction between *performer* and *originator* is needed precisely for the purpose of accounting for corporate linguistic activity. In spoken advertising, there is at least the distinction between the person who writes the copy and the person who speaks it. Normally many other people are involved, and rather than trouble to identify each, we can be content to say that the message has a 'collective source'. The same is true of a great deal of broadcast and printed language.

Communications are of collective origin in another sense when they are made *on behalf of* a corporate body. Official communiqués are issued by 'Foreign Office spokesmen'; business letters are dictated and signed by people in their capacities as Managers, Secretaries, Information Officers, and so on.

There is, therefore, some measure of 'publicness' at both the initiating and receiving end of a linguistic message. But to my mind, the public situation *par excellence* is that for which neither origin nor destination are specifiable; where the individual source and address are altogether irrelevant to the message, and the text has an institutional existence independent of participants. In written language, this circumstance is familiar; many Government records, official documents, and Stationery Office publications apparently have no author, and are simply addressed to whom they may concern. They originate from 'the Government' – an abstract, rather than a collective noun. Dictionaries, encyclopaedias, and other reference books compiled by corporate labour and emended through the years often attain a comparable anonymity of authorship, at least in the eyes of the public which uses them. Perhaps spoken English approaches nearest to this degree of anonymity in the B.B.C. news bulletins.

Formal English, with its overtones of dignity and authority, has often been esteemed and emulated as if it had inherent virtues regardless of context. This attitude can be responsible for an inept use of the formal style, resulting in obscurity, pomposity and circumlocution. But in recent years, partly through the efforts of Sir Ernest Gowers (the author of *The Complete Plain Words*) and other writers, there has been something of a stylistic reform. Formal English has lost ground in many spheres of public communication; in commerce, journalism, and even in Government departments. However, it remains unchallenged in science and the law – in these registers there are special problems of communication for which a colloquial style is quite unsuitable.

In part, the movement of 'colloquialisation' is merely an extension of a process which has been going on during the past hundred years through the advent of general literacy and education, and through the growth of media of mass communication. This is the evolution of a popular style of communication which might be called PUBLIC-COLLOQUIAL, since it has all the main features of colloquial English, despite the fact that it generally has a collective origin and is addressed to a large audience. Advertising has long been in the vanguard of this tendency, which has gained impetus in this century particularly through the development of the popular press and radio and television broadcasting.

The rise of this public-colloquial style can be ironically attributed to the enormous size of audiences which can now be reached by direct linguistic communication: mass audiences unimaginable before general literacy and broadcasting. Formal English is 'difficult' both because it is the style which has to be acquired *after* colloquial English, largely through formal education, and because it is the vehicle of precise and rational expression. For this reason, a colloquial style is naturally favoured when the originator's aim is to make contact with 'the general public', regardless of standards of education.

Here is an example of advertising copy which illustrates some typical features of colloquial English:

> Think about all this. And ask yourself – isn't it worth finding out more about it? Of course it is. And there is no time like the present – so get that pen out now, and fill in the coupon right away. Or call in and talk things over at your nearest R.A.F. Careers Information Centre.

To highlight the relevant points, I shall attempt a free 'translation' of this passage into more formal English:

> Ponder the above information, and consider whether it will not repay further investigation. Of course it will; and since there is no time like the present, take a pen now and complete the coupon immediately. Otherwise, visit your nearest R.A.F. Careers Information Centre and discuss the question there.

This 'translation' is awkward and slightly ludicrous, because it still incorporates features (for example, imperatives and the substitute verbal group 'it *will*') which, whilst I would not classify them as colloquial, tend to accompany a colloquial style. Also, there is a certain precision in formal discourse which can only be attained by departing from the original message. 'There is no time like the present', for instance, is a quasi-proverbial expression in informal conversation, containing an idiomatic and typically colloquial use of the word *like* following a negative. *Like* here has the force of 'as good as', 'as favourable as', etc.; and such implied meanings would generally be made explicit in formal English. To find a satisfactory formal equivalent for this whole expression, we would have to 'rethink' the idea in terms of the formal style.

This passage abundantly illustrates one characteristic of colloquial English: the use of 'phrasal verbs', consisting of a verb (usually one of very high frequency and unspecific meaning, such as *get, take, put*) and a pre-

positional adverb: *find out, get* . . . *out, fill in, call in, talks (things) over.*
In formal English, the preference is for a single verb of more specific
meaning; *discover, ascertain,* and *investigate* are all possible formal equivalents of *find out.* Grammatically speaking, *think about* does not belong to
this category, as *about* is a preposition, requiring a nominal complement
(*it* in the passage). But the same kind of observation applies to this
phrase: single transitive verbs in a more formal style, such as *encounter,
attack, enter,* have approximately the same semantic function as colloquial
combinations of verb and preposition: *come across, go for, go/get into.* The
word *get* and the negative contraction of *isn't* are obvious colloquialisms,
and the conjunction *so* might be added to them; I have avoided it in the
formal version by making the preceding clause a dependent clause of
reason.

Casual-ceremonial

This dimension of style operates only in private discourse, but it has an
interesting indirect bearing on advertising language.

Our manner of talking to one another, in ordinary conversation,
depends to a considerable extent on (*a*) the degree of intimacy between
between participants, and (*b*) the degree of superiority or inferiority of
status (if any) separating the speaker from the addressee. These two contextual factors are bound to the same set of linguistic variables: the languages of respect and condescension differ from one another in the same
way as do the languages of remoteness and familiarity. It is well known
that in some European languages the speaker has to make a choice, on
either of these grounds, between familiar and polite pronouns of address
(French *tu* and *vous*; German *du* and *Sie*).

Such choices do not arise in formal language, which is for obvious
reasons orientated towards the polite or 'ceremonial' end of the scale.
Indeed, it might be asked whether there is any need to separate the two
dimensions. Why should not the 'formal' and 'ceremonial' styles be
identified with each other, and the casual style be considered the extremity
of colloquialism? One answer is that the most ceremonial type of English
has characteristics which are not paralleled at all in formal English: for
example, the almost mandatory use of vocatives ('Yes, Mr. Smith';
'Quite so, my lord'; 'No, madam'). Also, at the other end of the scale, the
casual type of English involves dialect restrictions: slang expressions limited to a small class of speakers; even private words and phrases having a

particular meaning only for the members of a family or a group of intimate friends.

The public-colloquial style is largely unaffected by this kind of stylistic variation. Broadcasters and journalists do not want to alienate their audiences by being either patronising or obsequious. Casual forms of language in particular are likely to be unfavourably received. Slang expressions associated with a limited social group will have a narrow appeal, and even slang more or less general to the community arouses widespread hostility – from those objecting to the propagation of what is considered 'bad English' via public media.

Except when composing monologues and dialogues for secondary participants, the copywriter normally steers a neutral course between casual and ceremonial language. There is an occasional exception to this rule when he is addressing a youthful audience. The following, which appeared in *Weekend*, a magazine of mainly teenage readership, is an unusually deep excursion into the casual range:

> *Headline:*   First again (It's getting a habit). The most 'with it' Jean ever offered on the market and the most exciting!
>
> *Body copy:*   The jean with the lowest rise – **but** the lowest – there isn't even room for hip pockets! Tight yet barrelled to 16. No one, but no one, can offer this Jean but **Modern Man** . . .

Even here the slang 'with it' is apologetically enclosed in inverted commas; and perhaps the copywriter is not so much descending to a familiar style as adopting a teenage jargon rather as a music-hall comedian adopts a 'stage-dialect'. It is a jocular affectation of slang.

One marginally casual feature of advertising language is the occurrence of what with rather inappropriate dignity has been termed PROSIOPESIS. In spoken language, a person often 'begins to articulate, . . . but produces no audible sound . . . till one or two syllables after the beginning of what he intended to say'.* What we hear is 'Just going for a walk' in place of 'I'm just going for a walk', or 'Found it?' in place of 'Have you found it?'. One way to describe this phenomenon is to say that certain initial elements have zero exponents; that is, they have no phonological representation (except perhaps for imperceptible movements of the vocal organs), but are nevertheless part of an occurring grammatical structure. In other words, they are silent, unvocalised elements of structure. The elements chiefly concerned are:

---

* Jespersen (1924), p. 310. 'Prosiopesis' is Jespersen's term.

1. *Subject of a clause*

   [It] fits in anywhere.

2. $\begin{cases} \textit{Subject} + \textit{first word of predicator} \\ \textit{Subject} + \textit{predicator} \text{ (if the predicator consists of a single word)} \end{cases}$

   [You'd] best go on to Guinness for a while and see for yourself.
   [Are you] sure there's enough?

3. *Determiner in an initial nominal group*

   [The] point is, your stuffing might cost you up to 2/- . . .

It is easy to postulate what the missing elements are; they are always grammatical words of low information value, and it is just because they are predictable that they can remain silent without risk of misinterpretation. People may condemn this as slovenly speech, but it cannot be criticised on grounds of communicative efficiency.

The above explanation might suggest that prosiopesis always occurs involuntarily, and in impromptu speech. This is untrue at least to the extent that it is widespread also in *imitations* of impromptu speech, particularly in fictional dialogues of the kind found in detective and adventure stories. In fact my impression is that writers of popular fiction tend to overdo this trick, interlarding their dialogues with such remarks as 'Sounds crazy' or 'Got that?', which impart to them a terseness rarely attained in real life conversation. This practice, as one might expect, extends to the fictional dialogues and monologues of advertising. But more noteworthy is the occurrence of prosiopesis in direct address advertising, both in the press and on television. All except one of the above examples are from direct address copy. It is especially common in *Yes/No* questions: 'Feeling low?'; 'Choosing motor-car parts?'. Indeed, on the evidence of my sample, this truncated variant of the *Yes/No* question is preferred, where a reasonable choice exists, to the more 'correct' form, in which subject and auxiliary verb are vocalised. That prosiopesis occurs at all in direct address advertising is an indication of a tendency to go beyond colloquialism in simulating the conditions of friendly, personal communication.

There is one apparent exception to the rule that the copywriter avoids extremes of familiarity. The R.A.F. advertisement quoted earlier contained six imperatives in less that sixty words: *think, ask, get, fill in, call in, talk things over.* This form of the verb is persistently used in both printed and broadcast advertising, and is rarely accompanied by a formula of politeness. In most private contexts such bald directives would seem intolerably rude; even the word *please*, added before or after the request, often falls below the required standard of deference, and we have to use question or statement forms, draping our demands in elaborate peri-phrases: 'Would you kindly . . .?', 'Perhaps you would be good enough to . . .', 'I wonder if you would mind . . .', etc. How is it that the copy-writer is able to take such apparently unresented liberties with his audi-ence? The answer is that the imperative in public communication does not suffer from the implication of its use in private contexts. We are used to receiving exhortations and directives in the imperative mood from all manner of public sources: road signs ('Halt at major road ahead'); public transport notices ('Do not lean out of the window'); instructions from Government departments ('Enter the full earnings . . . for the year ended 5 April, 1964'). In this respect, we are more conditioned to bare imperatives than citizens of some other countries – for example, France, where officialdom can employ the more oblique infinitive: 'Ne pas se pencher au dehors' ('Not to lean out [of the window]').

The conditions under which *please* accompanies the imperative in messages addressed to the general public reflect a cynicism no doubt shared by anyone who has to regulate or manipulate mass behaviour. The word is used when the appeal is at least partially to our better feelings, and omitted when we are invited to consult our self-interest (including our interest in complying with demands which others have the power to enforce). In one compartment of a London tube train, two painted notices read 'Keep clear of the doors' and 'Do not alight from moving train', whereas a poster bore the more polite message 'Please avoid rush hour travel'. I have found only one example of *please* in direct address to the viewer in television advertising:

> But if your D.E.R. set *should* need attention, please ring us as early in the day as possible.

Here the advertiser is in the unwonted situation of asking for the con-sumer's co-operation. In press advertising, the politer exhortation is uncommon, except in charity advertisements ('Please give generously'). Its implication is that the advertiser is asking a favour of his readers, instead of doing them a favour (as he would normally like it to appear).

Personal-impersonal

A personal style is marked by free use of first person and second person reference, and sometimes also of forms of language (e.g. imperatives, questions, exclamations) which involve the first and second persons without direct reference. In a thoroughly impersonal style, on the other hand, first and second person pronouns will not be used at all; instead, there will be special third person forms which are in effect devices for evading reference to author and addressee. The passive voice can be a way of avoiding the specification of a first or second person subject. Constructions such as 'We hope that . . .', 'To my mind . . .', 'You will agree . . .', can be replaced by 'It is hoped . . .', 'It appears that . . .', 'It must be conceded . . .', etc. Nouns in the generic singular ('the reader'; 'the applicant') or unspecific plural ('customers'; 'residents') can be substituted for *you*. Thus an official might explain over the telephone, 'We want you to send the examination fee . . .', but the printed instruction will read, 'Candidates are asked to send the examination fee . . .' The following footnote from a contractor's estimate is a fair specimen of impersonality of style:

> NOTE. – No servants in the employ of the contractors are allowed under any circumstances to solicit gratuities, and in the event of any solicitation, incivility, or negligence of duty on their part, the Contractors will feel extremely obliged by its being reported to them by letter.

The fact that the style of this note is also extremely *formal* raises the question of how far impersonality of style is dependent on the other stylistic dimensions we have considered. First of all, impersonality can be virtually excluded from private discourse: only in a few stereotyped contexts of extreme ceremoniousness is third person address and self-reference still used: 'The right honourable gentleman is no doubt aware . . .'; 'Mrs. Bernard Twentyman requests the pleasure of . . .'. In public discourse, impersonality is associated with anonymity of participants, and therefore with the upper end of the formality scale. But in less formal contexts, no generalisation can be made about impersonality as a single dimension; separate consideration has to be given to impersonality *as regards first person* and impersonality *as regards second person*.

In advertising, impersonality as regards first person depends on whether the aim is to publicise a business or firm, or to publicise a consumer commodity. In prestige advertising, *we* is a common means of referring to the advertiser. In consumer advertising, the advertiser is generally referred to by name, in the third person: *Addis, Mackintosh's* etc.; *I* and *we* are almost entirely confined to the speech of secondary participants.

In other words, prestige advertising is predominantly personal, and consumer advertising predominantly impersonal as regards the first person. Both types are personal as regards the second person, and in this they are typical of the public-colloquial style.

The frequency with which first and second person reference occurs is a different matter, depending on the topic and the role of the message. For example, if the second person pronoun is rarely used in popular newspaper reports, it is not because the writer wants to avoid it, but because he has little call to use it: the reader is not part of his subject-matter. The copywriter, on the other hand, has every reason to use it, as the consumer (whom he is addressing) is one of the two principal topics of advertising – the other being whatever is being advertised (product or business concern). The importance of second person reference in consumer advertising can be gauged from the fact that in my television sample, 3 per cent of all words were occurrences of the second person pronoun and one in five of all independent clauses were imperative. In contrast, the advertiser is, it seems, rarely mentioned except as a means of identifying the product. It is significant that the passive voice, which is on the whole very rare in consumer advertising, freely occurs where to use an equivalent active clause would involve reference to those involved in the production of the advertised commodity: 'And Kraft Superfine is made from the purest vegetable oils'. (By whom? It is not the business of the advertisement to tell us.) This press advertisement shows the opposing tendencies of consumer advertising with regard to first person and second person reference:

[*Illustration*]

Headline: Only the rich, warm Australian sun and selected K-Y fruits can bring you such flavour

Body copy: You'll taste the sunshine in K-Y peaches, pears and apricots. Only K-Y fruit is ripened **on the tree** to capture the full, natural sunshine flavour of tree-fresh Australian fruit. K-Y fruits are picked and canned fresh from the orchard on the very same day.

Signature line: K-Y is your best buy!

The direct address to the reader (*you, your*) contrasts with the avoidance of reference to the producers in the passive voice with an unexpressed agent ('is ripened', 'are picked and canned').

Simple-complex

Complexity of language is not entirely a question of style: factors of subject matter or medium (for example, whether the text is spoken or written) are also highly relevant. But perhaps the most essential criterion for the appropriateness of a complex style is the status of the audience as regards age, education, and willingness to participate. It is a well-known, if lamentable, fact that our present society, as an audience for mass-media, tends to divide itself into two groups: the 'high-brows' and the rest.* The difference is most clearly seen in the split, in our national daily and Sunday newspapers, between the 'popular' and 'quality' grades, the *Daily Telegraph* and *Sunday Telegraph* being the only publications which attempt to 'fill the gap'. A good way to study complexity of style is to compare how the same news item is reported, say, by *The Times* and *The Daily Sketch*:

> Mr. Wilson, the Opposition leader, last night asked Sir Alec Douglas-Home in his capacity as First Lord of the Treasury for an urgent meeting to discuss the worsening situation in the postal workers' dispute and the union call made earlier in the day for all postmen and sorters to come out on official strike from Saturday midnight for an indefinite period . . .
>
> (*The Times*, 23 July, 1964)

> The Cabinet, faced with a strike-to-the-finish decision by 120,000 postmen, meets today to discuss a new peace formula. THE PLAN: To increase Postmaster-General Mr. Reginald Bevin's pay rise offer from 4 to at least 5 per cent . . .
>
> (*The Daily Sketch*, 23 July, 1964)

On the same page of *The Sketch* as this report is an advertisement illustrating the general rule that advertising material is simpler than news material in the same publication; this is partly because news reporting lends itself to a particular kind of linguistic complexity, and partly because advertising has to cater for a largely indifferent and unco-operative audience:

Headline: For **straight** pineapple juice drink a Britvic

[*Illustration*]

---

* See Williams (1962), pp. 58–62.

Body copy: Britvic is the name for **pure, undiluted** fruit juices
bottled straight from the fresh fruit.

Signature line: You can't beat the real thing!

We can give the notion of 'complexity' a precise linguistic meaning by
equating it with the number of elements of structure per grammatical
unit. For example, having described the structure of the clause in English
in terms of four elements – Subject (s), Predicator (p), Complement (c),
and Adjunct (a) – we can say that four clauses expounded by respectively
2, 3, 4, and 6 elements of structure are in order of increasing complexity:

S P	I know
A S P	There they go
S P C C	I've brought you a present
A S P C A A	Tomorrow I shall send him home again

One further step, that of computing the average number of elements per
clause, takes us to a measure of the complexity of a *whole text* in respect of
clause structure. However, there is no reason why the clause should be
singled out above other units as a gauge of complexity. A complete
measure of grammatical complexity would require a similar calculation
for all non-minimal units: word, group, clause, and sentence. It would
also require us to take account of depth-ordered structure (co-ordination,
dependence, embedding) as well as the place-ordered structure represented
above.

The number of words per sentence and the number of morphemes
(stems and affixes) per word have sometimes been accepted as satisfactory
standards of complexity. These formulae are, indeed, useful, and as
thorough as is normally practicable. But the word-per-sentence measure
in fact telescopes three separate steps: the number of words per group;
the number of groups per clause; and the number of clauses per sentence.
These separate steps happen to be relevant to the present study, because,
as we shall see, most of the complexity of advertising language is found in
group structure (in fact in the structure of the nominal group). Grammatical structure at other ranks is on the average exceptionally simple.

Chapter 9
Mode of Discourse

We turn now to a discussion of how language varies according to the medium of transmission. An obvious starting point is the contrast between auditory and visual transmission; that is, between speech and writing. No contrast of situation could appear more clear-cut than this one, and yet if we bear in mind the distinction between the origin and performance of a message there is room for indeterminacy. The transmission of the message is a question of performance alone; therefore the 'same message' may be performed in two different media. Any spoken utterance may be transcribed to some degree of accuracy, and even a mathematical formula can be given a spoken performance. In a way, such performances alter the message itself; for example, in reading aloud, we are forced to make linguistic choices (of intonation, etc.) for which the text does not provide. Yet it remains substantially the 'same message'.

Because of this difficulty, it is necessary to separate the *primary* medium of performance from incidental performances having no bearing on the form of language used. It is possible to find cases in which even the primary medium is in doubt (e.g. that of a poem intended equally for reading and spoken performance); but these are rare enough to be ignored. Subsidiary performances in a different medium may be 'pre-performances' (scripting in the case of speech, and dictation in the case of writing), or 'post-performances' (transcription in the case of speech, and reading aloud in the case of writing). The only one of these which is important for register is script writing. It also happens to be important for this study, as virtually all spoken advertising is scripted. The three categories of medium with which we are initially concerned are therefore

> spoken only
> written only
> written to be spoken (scripted).

Spoken, Written and Scripted Modes
The spoken-written dichotomy has an obvious correlation with the colloquial-formal dimension of style. As soon as we put pen to paper, we

are psychologically confronted with the relative permanence of the written record, and with the theoretical possibility of our message reaching a wide audience. But when written communication is of a purely private nature, we make few concessions to formality. Personal letters generally have all the characteristics of the colloquial style.

The most significant property of the written word, with regard to register, is indeed its *preservation through time*; but the important implications are not those mentioned above. From the second person's point of view, it means an opportunity to refer backwards and forwards from one part of the message to another – to escape from the temporal successivity which tyrannises over the spoken medium. From the first person's point of view, it means an ability to plan, revise, and rehearse the message before performance. This privilege is theoretically available in the spoken medium, but keeping one's mouth shut until the message is exactly planned is scarcely a practicable procedure in conversation.

One factor which affects the assimilation of a spoken message is the limited capacity of the linguistic memory. We should, indeed, rather speak of a number of different factors, as the expression 'linguistic memory' can refer to several different faculties: for example, it might mean either the ability to recall the substance of a speech by paraphrase or summary, or the ability to recall it word by word. Disillusioned public speakers complain that a point must be repeated a number of times before an audience can be assumed to have grasped it. 'Repetition' here means 'saying the same thing in different words'. Advertising practitioners, on the other hand, have an eye on the higher goal of verbatim recall. It is desirable that the audience should remember at least the name of the advertised product, and possibly also some catch-phrase which goes with it. This is a reason for using exact verbal repetitions, together with other features of mnemonic value, such as rhyme and alliteration.

I wish to give particular attention, however, to 'memory' in a more restricted sense: to the short-term memory by which grammatical elements in sequence are stored until the anticipations they create are resolved.* Regressive dependent clauses such as 'If you agree . . .' and pre-modifications such as 'the only . . .' are examples of 'incomplete' structures – structures which, to make grammatical sense, require complementation by at least one further element (an independent clause and a nominal head respectively). Similarly, the subject of a clause presupposes

---

* These ideas on the immediate memory span are based very loosely on Yngve (1961).

the addition of at least a predicator. The fragment 'If the only . . .' is incomplete at three ranks: it is an incomplete sentence consisting of an incomplete clause containing an incomplete nominal group. Suppose this forms the beginning of a sentence completed as follows: 'If the only train is the 2.42, let's go by bus.' The expectations arising from the first three words are satisfied by the word *train* (completing the group), the verb and complement 'is the 2.42' (completing the clause), and the independent clause 'let's go by bus' (completing the sentence). One way of understanding the terms 'expectation' and 'satisfaction' is to postulate a mental mechanism of storing anticipatory elements until the units of which they are part can be comprehended retrospectively, as a whole. At any point, the extent to which the temporary memory is brought into play depends on the number of incomplete structures, and the number of elements stored. As the latter figure increases as one goes up the rank scale, the memory is most burdened by anticipations in the units of clause and sentence. A sentence which begins *If as soon as the person whose* . . . will be difficult to follow not only because of its complexity, but also because it places a strain on the temporary memory. The difficulty is for the speaker, as well as the hearer. Someone who begins a sentence in this ambitious way is all too likely to end up by mixing his constructions, or stuttering to a halt.

Of course it is possible to avoid taxing the memory unduly by using different constructions which express approximately the same meaning. Two or more sentences can take the place of one; dependent clauses can be placed after the main clause instead of before, or alternatively a co-ordinative link can be used. Speakers prefer to place the 'meat' of a clause after the predicator, and the typical spoken sentence is the opposite of the 'periodic' sentence which is the traditional model for written prose.

It is symptomatic of the difference between speech and writing that some degree of editing is almost always considered necessary when a spoken discourse is published in written form. In the case of extempore speech, the text has, of course, to be rid of hesitations, false starts and the like. In both extempore and rehearsed speech, it is often desirable to generally 'tidy up' the text, by omitting temporisers such as *Well* . . . , *You see* . . . , *What I think is* . . . , asides, and incidental remarks which are aids to spoken communication, but are superfluous in print. However, a recent development in weekly newspapers and reviews has been the publishing of interviews with apparently the very minimum of editing, and a passage from one of these (an interview with the Beatles in *The Observer*) will provide a fairly true picture of unpremeditated speech:

No, I really don't feel like one . . . I really don't . . . that is, I don't feel like I imagine an idol is supposed to feel. Well, anyway, today this woman came up to the car; she'd never go up to just *anybody* in the street and kiss them, I mean she was just sort of talking to me and she suddenly grabbed hold of me and kissed me, I mean I was definitely embarrassed.

The three-fold repetition of 'don't feel', the temporising phrases 'well anyway', 'I mean', 'sort of' – all these are very characteristic of the spoken medium, in that one of their functions is a non-communicative one – that of 'playing for time' under the pressure of extempore performance. The passage also shows a minimum of grammatical anticipation at the ranks of clause and sentence.

The ordinary type of transcription gives an imperfect picture of the spoken language both because it eliminates hesitations and similar phenomena, and because punctuation can only represent a small part of the richness of meaning conveyed by intonation. In this passage, the italicising of *anybody* is one instance of an attempt to capture graphically something of the expressive power of intonation. In phonological terms, it indicates the position of the nucleus of an intonation pattern; that is (roughly), a point of major emphasis, at which stress coincides with a decisive change of pitch. The neutral position of the nucleus (NEUTRAL TONICITY) is on the last important word in the stretch of language spanned by the intonation pattern (SENSE-GROUP). In effect, this is the last word of the sense-group apart from 'grammatical words' such as prepositions, pronouns, and auxiliary verbs. But the nucleus may be shifted to an earlier, or even later position if (for example) the speaker wants to give contrastive prominence to some other part of the sense-group. In the sentence 'What are you looking for?' the neutral position of the nucleus is on *looking*; but it is not difficult to imagine a context for each of these four variants with MARKED (or special) TONICITY:

What are you looking for?
What *are* you looking for?
What are *you* looking for?
What are you looking *for*?

Devices of graphic emphasis such as underlining and italics can be used to represent special tonicity in speech, but they rarely perform this function consistently. In the passage quoted, for example, there was almost certainly an unrecorded special nucleus on *imagine* or *supposed*. In formal written English, the use of graphic emphasis for this kind of purpose is avoided; indeed, one of the skills of writing formal English consists in arranging one's ideas so as to make the end of each sense-group (as indicated by punctuation) as far as possible the appropriate place for emphasis. If neutral tonicity is employed throughout, emphasis is implicit in punctuation, and the reader's task is easier.

So far my remarks about the spoken language have applied mainly to unrehearsed and unscripted speech. Scripted speech is in many ways intermediate between this and written language. Obviously it does not characteristically have those features of speech (such as hesitations) which derive from spontaneity of performance. But from the listener's point of view, the limitations of the medium are the same: he cannot scan back over a sentence which has just been uttered, as if a tape repeater were built into his brain. In a script well adapted to the spoken medium, anticipatory structure will be used sparingly. With respect to tonicity, there is no theoretical reason why the expressive power of the shifted nucleus should not be fully exploited in scripted speech; yet in practice, it is probably used a great deal less than in ordinary conversation. The scriptwriter is naturally under the influence of the written mode; he is inclined to be parsimonious with signals of graphic emphasis, and to leave it to the script-reader to improvise special tonicity where it is called for.

The advertising announcer is one type of script-reader who cannot be accused of ignoring the value of tonicity. The sound-tracks of television commercials are liberally scattered with shifted nuclei, often, like the three examples in the following extract, at places where the script is unmarked:

No *other* rubbing, Swift does the work *for* you. No, no, no! Leave it! No rinsing. Swift is a *complete* carpet shampoo.

In the scripts, underlining is used not only for special tonicity, but also for other forms of emphasis, rendered by extra loudness, extra high pitch, measured rhythm, etc. It is interesting that the announcer not only introduces his own shifted nuclei but ignores some which are indicated by the script. In this, spoken advertising reflects the general casualness with which stress and intonation are handled in scripted language. They tend to be treated as something external to the message, having no important communicative function.

A word about a possible confusion between scripted and fictional speech: that is, between 'language written-to-be-spoken' and 'language written-(or scripted)-as-if-spoken'. There is no real connection between these categories, except that both are, in a sense, speech 'tidied up' – speech lacking the redundancies and anomalies of ordinary conversation. Fictional speech belongs to secondary situations (dialogues and monologues) in both written and spoken advertising: it includes dramatised conversations and invented testimonies on behalf of the advertised product. It is a direct simulation of extempore speech, and reflects its character in the measure that dramatic realism is desirable.

Disjunctive and Abbreviated Grammar

Here we broaden our concept of medium to include the extent to which language is accompanied by other means (particularly visual means) of communication, and how language is affected by the restrictions on transmission as regards speed, time and space. The DISJUNCTIVE and ABBREVIATED modes are two relatively restricted varieties of English with an important bearing on advertising language. The abbreviated mode is included in the disjunctive mode, and both are distinguished from the DISCURSIVE mode of ordinary connected discourse by peculiarities of grammatical structure.*

The disjunctive mode belongs to contexts in which, for one reason or another, the message is of an abnormally simple nature, much of its import being inferred from the circumstances in which it is transmitted. Some of these contexts are:

> Public notices, signs, and signposts
> Posters
> Catalogues, inventories, and other tabulated materials
> Postal addresses
> Labels and trade-marks
> Titles and headings

The abbreviated mode belongs to a narrower range of contexts in which a high premium is placed on the physical brevity of the message in terms of time or space. It is used, for example, in telegrams and newspaper headlines.

In disjunctive English, situational factors (often including factors of

---

* For previous explorations of this little studied area of grammar, see Straumann (1935), and Leech (1963).

visual lay-out,) afford so many clues to correct interpretation that the referential explicitness of discursive communication can be dispensed with. Imagine four doors bearing the notices 'AVONLEA', 'J. JONES', 'STAFF ONLY' and 'NO EXIT'. All these legends are grammatically alike, in that they are made up of single noun groups. But by a combination of convention and inference from the situation we are able to interpret them quite differently: 'This house is called "Avonlea"'; 'This office belongs to J. Jones'; 'This entrance is for staff only'; 'This door is not an exit'. The form of the discursive gloss is, in part, arbitrary: 'J. Jones works in here' or 'This is J. Jones's office' would do just as well for the second notice. There is no question, then, of describing them as 'incomplete sentences' in a grammatical sense, as there is no way of deciding what particular elements have been omitted. Instead of measuring disjunctive grammar against 'full' (discursive) grammar and finding it wanting, we have to describe it as it is.

The best way to approach it is to start with the very simplest ('most disjunctive') type of message and to ask 'How much of English grammar is needed for its description?'

AVONLEA

J. JONES

LITTLEHAMPTON

IMPERIAL

These notices are merely naming labels, and to understand them, all we need is a knowledge of the structure of English proper names: i.e., one part of the nominal group.

NO ENTRY

STAFF ONLY

GENTLEMEN'S WASHROOM

ENQUIRIES AND APPLICATIONS FOR VISAS

These are examples of messages which utilise only nominal group structure. This type of disjunctive English is so common that it is useful to have a separate name for it: BLOCK LANGUAGE*. The extended use of

---

* Used in a rather wider sense by Straumann (1935), p. 21.

block language is characteristic of many types of public announcement:

Because of the introductory formula 'Associated British presents . . .'
(the beginning of a finite-verb clause), the noun groups just fail to have
the monopoly of this film announcement. It is typical in such cases as this
that structural relations are obscured and rendered unimportant by
visual display. It is only out of grammatical niceness that one would want
to decide what is the object of *presents*, or what are the two noun groups
linked by *plus*. To all intents and purposes, each noun group is an isolated
unit, and the relations between different parts of the message are inferred,
not grammatically indicated. One of the reasons for this is that in this
poster-like presentation, the principle of linguistic sequence is disregarded. The convention of left-to-right, top-to-bottom order is waived
for the sake of immediate visual impact.

Since we have already moved into the domain of advertising in its
broadest sense, we may take one step further and examine a slightly more

complicated variety of disjunctive grammar which is virtually unique to advertising:

for you this summer . . . a golden tan

This headline is in two sections, of which the first is an adverbial group, and the second a noun group. Since different classes of group are in operation, there is the possibility of considering their relation to one another in terms of clause structure. The whole headline can be characterised as an independent minor clause of the structure A z, just as 'at one time a royal residence' in

> The castle, at one time a royal residence, is now the property of the National Trust

is a dependent minor clause of the structure A z. This is a very simple kind of clause structure, but it calls for a grammar more complex than that of earlier illustrations, in which the ranks of clause and sentence were dispensed with altogether.

Finally, we move to a type of disjunctive language in which some account has to be taken of sentence structure:

You

. . . if you are aged 16–19 and are taking or have passed your G.C.E. . . .

and your future

In this headline, the *if* clause is clearly dependent on the initial 'you', so 'you' is functioning as an independent minor clause, and consists of a single element z. 'Your future', being co-ordinated with 'you', also has to be taken as an independent clause. This example brings into play all five ranks of English grammar, yet it still differs essentially from discursive English, in that it contains minor clauses in independent function.

This brings us to the crux of the difference between discursive and disjunctive grammar: *in fully discursive grammar*, minor and non-finite clauses are dependent; *in fully disjunctive grammar* they are independent. This one statement accommodates all the simplifications of grammar that have been illustrated. It means, in effect, that in disjunctive language a sentence need not contain a finite predicator, and this in turn means that a single nominal group or a single adverbial group may be grammatically independent. Either of these groups may in turn consist of a single word. In other words, there is no limit to the simplicity of a grammatical unit. But to the extent that the higher units of grammar are left unexploited, they can be disregarded in description. In block language, for example, a nominal group is effectively equivalent to a sentence: grammatical description requires no reference to higher units.

The abbreviated mode is, following the definition above, a sub-category of the disjunctive mode: it has a special repertoire of non-finite and minor independent clause types, which can be illustrated from the following headlines (from *The Times* of 23 July, 1964). In the structural formulae, 'P_n' stands for a non-finite predicator:

Curfew | renewed | in silent Singapore	S P_n A
Riots death toll | now | eight	S A C
Newspaper | to hand | over | photograph	S P_n A C
Tory Political Centre chief | leaving	S P_n

On the face of it, this type of grammar lends itself more than those previously illustrated to description in terms of 'omissions'. It might be described as 'ordinary grammar' (i.e., discursive grammar) with items of low information value left out. By inserting such elements as the verb *to be* and the definite or indefinite article, we arrive at sentences which look fairly presentable specimens of orthodox discursive English:

The curfew has been renewed in silent Singapore
The riots death toll is now eight

But this second sentence gives a clue to another structural peculiarity of abbreviated grammar (particularly the variety used in headlines). Pre-modifying nouns are used with far greater freedom than is usual. A *completely* discursive rendering would only be obtained by a syntactical rearrangement as follows:

'The riots death toll' = 'the death toll in the riots'
                       = 'the toll of deaths in the riots'

'Tory Political Centre chief' in the fourth headline might similarly become 'A (*or* The) chief of the Tory Political Centre'. The difficulty over choice of article here is a matter of ambiguity. In 'Newspaper to hand over photograph', however, I feel that neither 'The newspaper' or 'A newspaper' would be strictly appropriate. This ambivalence as regards definite or indefinite meaning is unparalleled in discursive English. The infinitive as it occurs in this sentence is also a special feature of abbreviated grammar: it has the value of a future tense, and does service for a variety of discursive forms: 'is to . . .', 'is going to . . .', 'will . . .', etc. All these points indicate that abbreviated English is not just discursive English with a few 'missing words'; it has to some extent an independent grammar of its own.

In some contexts (for example, note-taking at a lecture) abbreviated grammar mingles with other types of disjunctive grammar. In a typical 'small ad', block language combines with the characteristic non-finite clause structures of the abbreviated mode:

> EXPERIENCED heading pipe fitters/
> fitter welders; London and country
> work; top rates paid; fares home paid
> fortnightly. – Phone HIT 9144.

A similar mixture is often found in display advertisements in local and other small-circulation publications:

CROUCH END MOTORS LTD.
YOUR LOCAL AGENTS FOR
AUSTIN ★ *MORRIS* ★ *FORD*
ANY MAKE OF CAR SUPPLIED
H.P. TERMS GLADLY ARRANGED

---

50   COLERIDGE   ROAD,   N.8
Telephones MOUNTVIEW 1845 and 1900

The two abbreviated clauses are 'Any make of car supplied' (structure: $s \, P_n$) and 'H.P. terms gladly arranged' (structure: $s \, A \, P_n$); the rest of the advertisement is pure block language.

Advertising copy, indeed, is a variety of English in which discursive, abbreviated, and block language are sometimes inextricably mingled together. The border-line between discursive and block language, in printed matter, is generally clear-cut, and coincides with the difference between running text and typographically isolated sections, such as headings, titles, and lists. This typographical distinction is often blurred by the variety of display methods and type-faces of printed advertising; the corresponding linguistic distinction is also difficult to make. Disjunctive language is primarily associated with headlines, subheads, and signature lines, and is therefore particularly prominent on poster advertising and television 'supers'. But it is also prevalent in body copy, where on purely typographical grounds one would not expect it. As for the abbreviated mode, this is found nowadays mainly in small-scale retail and personal advertising. But this is not to exclude it altogether from large-circulation advertising, where it occurs in various subsidiary functions: notably in standing details.

So far this description of disjunctive grammar has been illustrated from the written language. To find examples from the spoken language, we would have to look no further than the brief, verbless remarks which are part of the small change of conversation: 'Good'; 'Cheers'; 'Ready?' 'Your go'. Sports commentaries are also rich in disjunctive features: 'Up the final straight with Britten in the lead . . . and now over to John Windsor at the finishing line.' And broadcasting seems to have developed its own varieties of block language, on the analogy of headings and lists on the printed page: for example, news headlines ('The situation in Cyprus') and sports results ('Racing at Bath; 2.30, Simtim, Wilmidge, Hoe Hill . . .').

In television advertising, the tendency to use disjunctive language is even stronger, if anything, than in press advertising. The shorter commercials (seven and fifteen seconds) often contain a kind of block language which suggests transposition to the spoken medium of habits acquired in, and applicable to, the medium of print:

> Addis. The paintbrush with the name you know.
> Addis.

As the amount of linguistic material in commercials of this length is severely limited, the technique employed is reminiscent of that of poster advertising. But longer commercials, too, sometimes have an endline which shows the influence of visual presentation: specifically, that of packaging displays and the trade-name-and-price captions of press advertising:

> Piccadilly – 4/2d for twenty.

Such is the power of combined visual and auditory impact in television that planners of commercials can afford to give speech a relatively minor role in the total communication. There are even commercials which contain no speech at all. The importance of the visual element of the total communication gives scope for a variety of disjunctive techniques, which will be illustrated in later chapters.

The abbreviated mode is rare in television copy, as it is in any form of spoken communication. But there are one or two examples in the shortest (seven-second) commercials:

> Don't miss great sale of Berkertex dresses.
> Hundreds at half-price. Tomorrow 9 a.m.

The abbreviated features here are the absence of the article before 'great sale', and of the preposition in 'Tomorrow 9 a.m.'

Chapter 10

Role of Discourse

The preceding sections on style and mode of discourse have gone some way towards characterising advertising English in relation to other roles of the language. It can be said, for example, that in comparison with scientific, legal, or business English, advertising English is extremely simple and colloquial; that it shares with popular journalism the 'public-colloquial' style; that it has (in its disjunctive component) some points of resemblance with the restricted languages of catalogues, road-signs, titles and so on. When all this has been said, we have to consider just what are the peculiarities of advertising English *as* advertising English rather than as a specimen of colloquial English, simple English, and so forth.

Role Specialisation

Every role has its own peculiar idiom. Scientific English has morphological monstrosities like *spectrophotometer*; legal English has its *undersigneds* and *hereinafters*; religious English has its *thous* and *untos*. These items are so strongly associated with particular roles that when we hear them out of context, they immediately strike us as 'scientific' or 'legal' or 'religious', as the case may be. Special vocabulary is only one aspect of language adapted or specialised to social function; there are also peculiarities of phonology, grammar, and semantics. All such features can be brought under the general heading of ROLE SPECIALISATION. Roles divide broadly into 'conservative' and 'liberal' types: those in which all pressure is towards conformity to accepted linguistic conventions (as in law and religion), and those in which the main tendency is towards originality and inventiveness of thought and language. In the latter category belong roles which could broadly be said to involve 'creative writing'. It includes not only the purely aesthetic use of language, but any form of composition in which the author is at liberty to develop his individual character as a writer: humour, fiction, educational literature, etc. In such roles, linguistic specialisation is very slight, and, where it occurs, is dismissed by practitioners or critics in derogatory terms as 'humdrum', 'hackneyed', 'jargon', 'cliché', etc. An author's skill in such roles is measured not so much by his adherence to linguistic convention as his success in escaping from it.

Advertising language seems to be in a special category, in that its 'conservative' and 'liberal' tendencies are delicately balanced. The tendency to linguistic conformity is manifested in a type of language I shall call 'standard advertising English' – although this label is not meant to suggest an unimaginative application of rule, or anything so rigid as a formula for mechanical copywriting. The opposite tendency of linguistic non-conformity shows itself in many different ways: in the adoption of eccentric 'styles', in the invention of new words, in linguistic games and jokes, in fact in any way that is likely to stimulate curiosity and interest. It is of course only the linguistic aspect of one of the fundamental advertising strategies: that of claiming attention through the surprise or entertainment value of the advertisement. But if an advertisement is successful in attracting attention to itself, it is not necessarily successful by the only criterion of success known to the advertising profession – sales figures. There is some conflict between the aims of wooing the public and spurring the public to the right kind of response. Common reactions in the advertising world are 'Run-of-the-mill stuff, but it does its job', or alternatively 'Clever and original, but will it sell?' Standard advertising English, however tiresome and cliché-ridden, has its advantages and its advocates.

It is against this background that we appreciate the scope and limits of role specialisation in the English of advertising. No specialised features of the role need to be illustrated at this point, as Part II of the book is devoted to their description and exemplification. Novelty and unconventionality in advertising copy will be among the topics covered by Part III.

Role Borrowing

However, before we leave the subject of role, it is appropriate to consider one non-standard type of copy which consists in the direct borrowing of features from other roles.

I should make it clear that we are dealing with direct advertising, and not with any of the secondary situations described in Chapter 5. Secondary situations have their own roles (interview, testimony, domestic dialogue, etc.) which belong only indirectly to the advertising situation itself, so it is understood that 'role borrowing' in one sense takes place whenever a secondary situation occurs.

Role borrowing is the use in one role of linguistic features appropriate to another. In private colloquy, its intent may be comic or sarcastic (for example, children sometimes address one another in the classroom manner of a schoolteacher); in literature, it can serve various artistic purposes; in humorous writing or comedy entertainment, it is a form of parody. In advertising, role borrowing is just one aspect of the versatility of linguistic performance allowed within the situation.

Here is a thirty-second television script which, in its grammatical structure, copies the format of an official form or record card:

> Her name: Elizabeth Eldon.
> Symptoms: Constant tiredness.
> Cause: Night Starvation.
> Recommendation: Horlicks.
> Horlicks guards against Night Starvation.

The rhetorical effect of this lies in its terseness and seeming objectivity; it contrasts with other aspects of the commercial, which are highly emotive: a surrealist filming technique, a soft tone of voice, evocative sound and musical effects.

Role borrowing is often a form of disguise, or at least a means of decoying the public into taking notice of the sales message:

> The Royal Highland Gathering at Braemar. The most famous of all the Highland Games. Throwing the hammer here is champion William Anderson who, when he's not winning trophies, is a hard-working crofter . . .

So far, this commercial has all the appearance of a popular documentary. Three grammatical features are very uncharacteristic of advertising, and belong rather to popular journalism and news-reporting: the main clause inversion 'Throwing the hammer here is. . . .' which splits the predicator, and places the subject at the end; the attributive appositional 'champion William Anderson'; and the parenthetical clause 'when he's not winning trophies'. The illusion is destroyed as the commercial proceeds, and we learn that its hero's prowess lies not only in hammer-throwing, but in egg consumption:

> William Anderson knows he needs plenty of protein for this strenuous life, and he gets it from eggs . . .

A similar approach is found in press advertisements which treat the reader to a piece of instructive general knowledge, and then lead him on to the

selling proposition via some tenuous and often merely verbal link. Under
the heading 'Great Writers', in an advertisement for propelling pencils, a
portrait of Samuel Pepys is displayed, and the following information is
presented in a popular 'encyclopaedic' manner:

> Of England's heritage of great writers, Samuel Pepys is
> unrivalled in history for his intimate diary, written in personal
> shorthand, which remained undeciphered until 1825.

A liberal interpretation of 'great writers' brings the copywriter to his
selling point:

> Today W. H. Collins are instrumental in building a new
> heritage of 'great writers'.

This type of copy is best suited to a sophisticated readership, which is
supposedly well armed against direct sales talk, but which has its own
particular weakness: the compulsive reading habit.

Disguise in copywriting reaches its extreme in the 'chameleon technique' whereby an advertisement is made to resemble, both in language
and lay-out, a feature or article of the publication in which it appears. It
is required that the advertisement should declare itself in bold letters
to be a wolf in lamb's clothing, so the effect of the stratagem is only
momentary deception – an initial bid for the reader's attention. Making an
advertisement look like a feature is not difficult in some types of publication, particularly women's magazines, which have tended to adopt, for
all kinds of material, the freedom of visual presentation pioneered by
advertising.

Making an advertisement sound like a scientific report is more difficult
but seems no less attractive to the copywriter. The language of science is
very unsuitable for advertising purposes, for the simple reason that it is
largely unintelligible to the layman. The use of scientific terms in advertising is rather like name-dropping in social conversation: it serves to
impress rather than to inform one's audience. The word *science* itself or
one of its derivatives can be just as impressive and less baffling. Hence the
copywriter's partiality for such locutions as 'science tells us . . .', 'scientific
tests show . . .', and 'scientifically clean'.

Part Two Standard Advertising English

Chapter 11

Standard Advertising English: Preliminaries

It is appropriate that the middle portion of this book should be devoted to the heart of the matter before us: a description of how English is specialised to the role of advertising. The use of the word 'standard' in this connection has its limitations, so it is as well to begin with a specification (partly recapitulating previous remarks) of how it will be understood.

(*a*) On the positive side, describing role specialisation consists in noting what linguistic choices are made in advertising more frequently than elsewhere, and how *much* more frequently these choices are made.

(*b*) Role specialisation also has a negative side: the relative infrequency of certain choices, and the degree of their infrequency. For instance, words expressing doubt, such as *perhaps* and *probably*, are rare in advertising for the obvious reason that they tinge the sales message with inconclusiveness and equivocation, offending against the principle of 'positive' copy. However, modesty in advertising is not unknown; one television campaign in 1961 carried the slogan 'probably the finest butter in the world'. Such deviations are exceptions that prove the rule, since their success depends at least partially on their unexpectedness in the advertising situation.

(*c*) At the poles of relative frequency and infrequency are cases of absolute exclusion: where a feature is unique to advertising English, or conversely never occurs in advertising English, though found in other registers. I have argued in Chapter 7 that such cases are unreal, and that all-or-none statements cannot (except in a few very special cases) be made about register. Items like *Neolithic* and *colloids* might be thought to have a nil probability of occurrence in advertising, yet both have occurred in advertisements I have studied. And from the opposite point of view, it might seem that adjective compounds like *top-of-the-stove (cookery)* could not occur outside advertising (leaving aside citations such as the one just made). But this is in principle unverifiable. We have to be content with 'often' and 'seldom' in place of 'always' and 'never'.

(*d*) Standard advertising English, as we have seen above, is a relative concept. Some features are 'more standard' and some more 'non-standard' than others. If a specimen of advertising language is called 'standard copy', an additional relative notion is introduced: the degree to which a given *text* follows the most predictable patterns. A thoroughly standard piece of copy would simply be a string of advertising clichés from beginning to end. But many advertisements contain one or two novel features in otherwise conventional copy.

To clarify further the notion of standard advertising English, I add two cautions about how it is *not* to be interpreted.

(a) It is not a standard for judging good (i.e. successful) or bad (i.e. unsuccessful) copywriting.

(b) It is not associated with any particular copywriting strategy: for example, with 'reason why', 'emotive', or 'reminder' copy. Most of the typical aspects of advertising language to be discussed are 'general purpose' features which apply (though perhaps to different extents) irrespective of what selling approach predominates in the advertisement.

A Specimen

With these stipulations in mind, we move on to a representative piece of standard advertising English. (Orthographic sentences in the body copy are numbered for ease of reference.)

[*Illustration*]

Headline: For grown-ups only

Body copy: 1. If your eyes are grown-up – well, seventeen or over – they're ready to start learning. 2. And just this once . . . let's begin at the end with the newest eye cosmetic of all – Innoxa's Shadow Soft Eye Shadow. 3. Utterly new because this eye shadow acts like a cream powder and is brushed on to your lids . . . leaving a fine-spun glimmer as delicate and perfect as a butterfly's wing. 4. It's easy to apply the most expert shading; and because this eye shadow is powder-light, you can blend different colours on your lids. 5. If you prefer a different kind of eye make-up, Innoxa's Shadow Satin, too, has a brilliance to spare. 6. Creamy, glinting, glamorous, Shadow Satin spreads on your eyelids delightfully, leaving no oiliness – only pure and lovely colour. 7. Other lessons in loveliness – your eyes can learn them from Innoxa's Dramatic Block, Roll-on or Cream Mascara, and Dramatic Eye Liner.

Standing details: Shadow Soft Eye Shadow 9/3
               Shadow Satin Eye Shadow 6/0
               For the name of your nearest Innoxa retailer write or call at
               the Innoxa Salon, 170 New Bond St., London W.1.

Signature line: Innoxa for living loveliness

Appearing in a quality fashion magazine, *Harper's Bazaar*, the language of
this advertisement is more complex than that of the majority of press
advertisements, and far more so than that of the average television commercial. However, it contains a large number of typical advertising
features, which can be conveniently noted under the headings of Chapters
12 to 17.

Clauses. The *if* clause ('If your eyes are grown-up', 1) is a common
opening, which serves to single out the audience to which the advertisement applies, or to strike some personal 'chord' in the heart of the
appropriate type of consumer. A second *if* clause later in the body copy
(5) has a similar function: it heralds the introduction of a second product,
for a new category of consumer.

    An imperative clause in the standing details has a typical initial *for*
phrase: 'For the name of your nearest Innoxa retailer'.

    Illustrative of the disjunctive tendency of advertising copy are inde-
pendent minor clauses in the headline, standing details, and signature line,
and also in the body copy ('Utterly new . . . , 3; 'Other lessons in loveliness', 7).

Verbal groups. As is generally true of advertising, simple present tense
forms predominate in finite clauses (*are*, 1; *acts*, 3; *prefer*, 5; etc.).

    Can is by far the most common modal auxiliary in advertising language,
and the inclusion of a second person pronoun in the subject preceding *can*
is extremely common: 'you can' (4), 'your . . . can' (7).

Nominal groups. The extended brand-name 'Innoxa's Shadow Soft Eye
Shadow' (2) illustrates something of the bizarre and complex aspects of
the noun group in advertising.

    Characteristic constructions are the absolute superlative 'most expert'
(4) and the intensified superlative 'newest . . . of all' (2).

Words and compounds. *Fine-spun* (3) and *powder-light* (4) are instances of
what is perhaps more than anything else a hallmark of advertising
English: the adjective compound.

Cohesion and lack of cohesion. Symptoms of lack of cohesion (or explicitness of semantic connections) are the examples of apposition in 2 ('the newest eye cosmetic of all – Innoxa's Shadow Soft Eye Shadow') and of unlinked listing, or parataxis, in 6 ('Creamy, glinting, glamorous'). These are types of co-ordination in which the relationship between the elements is not signalled by a linking word.

Parataxis is combined with vertical display in the product-and-price listing in the standing details.

A tendency to rely on lexical rather than grammatical connections is seen in the repetition of *new* at the beginning of sentence 3. A reprise of *new* followed by a *because* clause is in fact something of an advertising cliché: the consumer is alerted with a promise of novelty, then given an explanation of what the novelty is.

Vocabulary. Apart from the double occurrence of the touchstone word *new*, we notice the amazing number and variety (for such a short text) of words of evaluative or evocative import: *delicate, perfect, expert, brilliance, delightfully, glamorous, lovely,* etc. Even the staid adjective *grown-up* is used with emotive effect.

To balance the picture, mention must be made of one or two respects in which this advertisement seems to be atypical. Although the adjective *new* and the superlative are individually very characteristic of advertising copy, the conjunction of these two features, as in 'the newest eye cosmetic of all' (2) is rare: *new* is generally taken to be absolute enough in meaning to require no extra intensification. The *because* clause 'because this eye shadow is powder-light' (4) is also unusual in that it precedes, rather than follows the main clause. However, a greater use of anticipatory dependent clauses is to be expected in the more complex kind of press copy. 'Leaving no oiliness' (6) goes counter to the general tendency of avoiding negation. But this is a special case: negatives are freely used in constructions where their effect is immediately cancelled out by a contrasting positive assertion, in this instance by 'only pure and lovely colour'.

Plan of Description

If the specimen analysis has given an idea of the range of topics to be covered, it may also have indicated that my account of standard advertising English will necessarily be selective. It will not be a formal textbook description designed for at least a superficial coverage of 'all the facts', but rather an attempt to present and comment on the most *significant* facts. The arrangement will resemble that of a dictionary with selected entries, rather than that of a compendious reference book.

Five chapters will deal with grammar, one with vocabulary, and one with semantics; but the compartmentalisation is not so rigid, nor the distribution of attention so unbalanced, as chapter headings suggest. The study of grammar and lexis are complementary ways of looking at linguistic form. Grammatical study involves starting with the most general and abstract patterns of language and moving to the more specific ones. Lexical study starts with the most specific entities – single items of vocabulary. The grammatical chapters will be largely concerned with the 'deepest' or most specific kind of grammar: the function of individual items within grammatical structures. This is the area where register differences are generally found. It is the area of 'advertising clichés' such as the occurrence of the verb *buy* in imperative clauses. For the chapter on vocabulary, there remains only the task of summarising gross facts about lexical items: a type of generalisation which could not be included in grammar.

The chapter on semantics similarly brings together generalisations about meaning which cut across grammatical and lexical patterns. If techniques of semantic description were sufficiently developed, this would no doubt be the proper place for the most interesting observations about advertising English and its relation to advertising motives. As it is, this chapter is best conceived of as a set of footnotes to the rest of the description.

Chapter 12

Clauses

Of the various clause systems described in the linguistic introduction (pp. 15–17), the system of mood (affirmative/interrogative/imperative) is one which calls for special comment. In private conversation, where there is free interchange of speaking and listening roles, all three types of clause have their respective functions. But in public communication, particularly in uni-directional media such as press and broadcasting, this is not the case. The selection of interrogative, and to a lesser extent, imperative clauses is restricted to special circumstances and special effects. Advertising English is exceptional in that it allows relatively free selection from the mood system: in the television sample, over one in thirty major independent clauses were interrogative, and over one in four major independent clauses were imperative.

Imperative Clauses

The very high frequency of imperatives in advertising is not a characteristic of other types of loaded language. As we saw in Chapter 8 (pp. 79–80), if the advertising imperative can be related to anything in other varieties of English, it is to the instructions and admonitions in public notices and official forms. However obvious it should seem that the copywriter should make lavish use of direct exhortations, they should be considered a conventional, rather than an inevitable feature of his repertoire.

Certain groups of verbal items are especially frequent in imperative clauses:

1. Items which have to do with the acquisition of the product. *Get* is by far the most frequent of these, and in fact of all imperative verbs: 'Get Super Snowcem'; 'Get the shave that's extra close – the Remington shave'; 'Get Andrex tomorrow'. Other items with a similar function are *buy* ('Always buy Cadbury's') *ask for* ('Always ask for Gallaher's Blues'); *choose* ('For the brightest gloss choose from Gaymel's wonderful colour range'). This kind of imperative is habitually addressed to the consumer: in the television sample it never occurred in dialogue situations, where a

secondary participant, not the viewing public, was being addressed. As a final urge to action it is a standard endline in television advertising.

2. Items which have to do with the consumption or use of the product, such as *have*, *try*, *use*, and *enjoy*: 'Have some Harveys with *your* Christmas'; 'Try new Rice Krispies'; 'Enjoy these chocolates that look divine'; 'For lovelier hairstyles use New Amami Waveset and Conditioner'.

3. Items which act as appeals for notice: 'While the Liberator heats the water, look at this'; 'Just see how marks and smudges disappear when you use Handy Andy'; 'Watch the Daxaids instant dispersal test'. *Look*, *see*, and *watch* are common in commercials of the 'demonstration' type, where they call the consumer's attention to what is happening before her eyes. *Remember*, *make sure*, and *see* (as in 'See that you too get enough milk') admonish her to learn a lesson for the future:

A very happy Christmas to all D.E.R. renters, and remember that our television service will be available throughout the Christmas Holiday.

As might be expected, prohibitive warnings like 'Don't let indigestion spoil your day' are very infrequent beside positive exhortations. Only about one imperative in fifty is accompanied by a negative form.

Interrogative Clauses

The distribution of interrogative clauses is the reverse of that of imperative clauses, in that they are more frequent in indirect than in direct address advertising. However, a question generally presupposes an answer, and in direct address the one-way channel of communication forbids an addressee to talk back. So we are led to ask why interrogatives are used at all in a situation where the originator must either leave his question unanswered, or answer it himself.

Interrogatives resemble imperatives in being stimuli which normally require an active response from the addressee: in the one case a verbal response, in the other case often a physical one.* In advertising, both may have the effect of stirring the consumer from her wonted state of passive receptivity. Questions, like commands, are frequent as headlines ('Are you going grey too early?'), and as the opening sentence of television commercials ('Choosing paint?'). To this kind of challenge consumers

---

* Questions have been classified as 'utterances regularly eliciting "oral" responses only' by Fries (1952), p. 53.

may be expected to return the mental answer 'Yes' or 'No', and those who answer 'Yes' are the people the advertiser wants to interest in his product. An interesting phenomenon of viewing behaviour confirms the success of this gambit in drawing the audience into some kind of active participation. Viewers annoyed at the interruption of an evening's entertainment will sometimes be heard to answer the opening question with an aggressive denial: 'Don't be silly, of course not', or words to that effect. This might cheer the copywriter on the grounds that 'any response is better than no response'; but whether apostrophising the television set has any correlation with buying the product is another matter.

Yes/No interrogatives which end in a falling tone, instead of the more usual rising tone, can be psychologically construed as exclamations: 'Isn't it marvellous stuff'; 'And don't they make a delightful display'. They express the speaker's enthusiasm and invite the listener's agreement. In direct address advertising, they indicate a simulation of a personal rapport between advertiser and consumer.

Wh- questions, which require a more specific answer than 'Yes' or 'No', are also quite common in advertising copy. When such a question is posed, the ensuing copy generally provides the answer:

> What's in *Woman's Realm* this week? A wonderful beauty offer for you.

> What's so special about Lurpak Danish butter? Well, can you remember what butter used to taste like – real fresh farmhouse butter? Do you remember how you used to enjoy it when you were young? Today – the taste of Lurpak brings it all back to you – that's why it's so special!

This extract illustrates a further type of *Yes/No* question: an appeal to the consumer to search his memory. Such questions have parallels in ordinary conversation: 'Do you remember Mrs. X? Well . . .'. In both cases an answer is not expected; or rather, the poser of the question does not really care if it is 'Yes' or 'No'.

The technique of exposition by question and answer is familiar in many kinds of discourse, particularly in those which aim to explain a complicated subject-matter in a relatively simple way. Psychologically, it may be a means of getting one's audience to grasp a point by presenting it in two separate stages: a problem, then its solution. Linguistically, it may be a means of reducing grammatical complexity, by expressing in two sentences what would otherwise have been most naturally expressed in one more complex sentence. Both these levels of interpretation apply in advertising, except that psychologically speaking, the question seems to be more of an invitation to the consumer to be curious about the information to be divulged. The effect of simplification can be judged by comparing the first example above with a single sentence paraphrase:

> There's a wonderful beauty offer for you in *Woman's Realm* this week.

This would be an acceptable alternative, but it contains unusual complexity of clause structure, with three adjuncts in succession (s p c a a a).

The 'rhetorical question', as classically understood, is not a feature of advertising copy, as it is of other types of persuasive language. This is the kind of *Yes/No* question which needs no verbal answer, and in addition has the force of an emphatically negative assertion:

> Does it seem to you to be sensible to treat this Company as a political football? Does the uncertainty which must then prevail help to recruit and keep the people we need? Is it right to keep those whom we employ, as well as those with whom we trade, in a state of continuing uncertainty?

The implied answer to these queries is a firm negative: 'No, I should think not' – which is just the kind of mental reply the copywriter's *Yes/No* questions are not intended to solicit. This is, in fact, an extract from an advertisement; but it is not advertising copy in the usual sense. It is part of an anti-nationalisation advertisement put out by a steel company in 1964, and is abstracted from a speech by the company's chairman. It is political oratory rather than advertising copy.

Non-finite and Minor Clauses

Non-finite and minor clauses (explained in the linguistic introduction, pp. 15–16) do not have 'mood', in the sense that they cannot be classified as either affirmative, interrogative or imperative. In fully discursive English, this would follow from their being automatically classifiable as dependent clauses. But in disjunctive advertising English, the situation appears to be almost the reverse: with the exception of embedded non-finite clauses (e.g. 'Now's the time *to think about it*') and very occasional minor clauses of the type introduced by a conjunction (e.g. 'when cold'), minor and non-finite clauses are almost invariably independent.

8—E.I.A.

The reason for suggesting such a grammatical divergence between discursive English and disjunctive advertising English is this: there are no reliable criteria for assigning minor and non-finite clauses to the dependent category, whereas both classes of clause readily fulfil the only positive criterion of independence: occurrence as a single clause within sentence structure. The chief signals of clause subordination in English are:

1. An initial subordinating word (*when, if, who*, etc.).
2. Parenthetical inclusion within another clause.
3. Intonation cues, such as a low rise or fall-rise pattern indicating dependence on a following clause.
4. Cues of punctuation paralleling those of intonation (e.g. a comma indicating dependence on a following clause).

The first of these criteria is unhelpful simply because most minor and non-finite clauses do not begin with a subordinating word. The second does not apply because parenthetical inclusion does not seem to occur in standard advertising English. In the television sample, there was only one instance of this construction, in copy which was quoted on p. 100 as a case of register borrowing – that is, of non-standard advertising language:

> Throwing the hammer here is champion William Anderson who, *when he's not winning trophies*, is a hard-working crofter.

The criteria of intonation and punctuation in general point to the independent status of minor and non-finite clauses. In disjunctive press body copy, for example, the comma is rarely used; and punctuation marks of greater separative force, full stops, dashes, and sequences of dots, predominate:

> 'A choice and unique blend' – as fine a promise of pleasure to come as you'll ever find. Escudo – a marvellous tobacco blended from just two kinds of leaf. Gold Virginia (actually grown in Virginia U.S.A.) and dark perique from Louisiana . . . cool-smoking discs of pure tobacco.

Occasionally there is an exception, where on grounds of punctuation or intonation a minor or non-finite clause can be held to be dependent on a following clause. This is the case with the initial non-finite clause of this television commentary (the clause was spoken with a fall-rise tone):

> Made from the whole wheat grain, Whole Wheat Flakes – Kellogg's New, delicious breakfast. Crisp flakes, crisp with the goodness of the whole grain, and a delicious taste that's new every morning.   And the zest of added vitamins to help your family to health . . .

Of course, there are varying degrees of 'disjunctiveness' in advertising copy. The two examples above represent the disjunctive extreme: they contain no main finite clauses, and would have perplexed (and probably horrified) a grammarian operating within the 'subject-predicate' tradition. As minor and non-finite clauses are generally very simple (the former have no predicator and the latter no subject), there is little structure above the group. This type of disjunctive language is not far removed in simplicity from block language (see p. 91). However, it draws on a greater variety of English grammatical structures, as noun groups are used in combination with adjective and adverbial groups. The mixture of noun and adjective groups, as in 'Cheese Dreams – so quick and yet so good', is as characteristic of disjunctive advertising language as is the mixture of minor and non-finite independent clauses. The most distinctive function of adverbial groups is in minor clauses with structures combining the elements A and z:

> Into this glass, washing powder. Into this one, soap flakes. Now, into this – new label improved Bubbly Stergene. (A z, A z, A A z)

> Love in your heart – peace in your mind – Lifeguard in your home – the disinfectant you trust completely. (z A, z A, z A)

Those clauses in which the adjunct precedes the nominal element (z) are not often found in other registers of English. Particularly characteristic are clauses whose initial adjuncts are prepositional phrases beginning with *for*:

> For quicker washing up, the Nylon Bridget and – the Pot Scrubber.

> For sturdy growth – for vitality – for beauty – and for relaxation – for sheer enjoyment – milk.

> For you – the golden crispness of Kellogg's Frosties.

Of the *for* phrases entering into these minor clause structures, some (e.g. 'for sheer enjoyment',) contain an abstract noun group signifying a benefit associated with the product, whereas others (e.g. 'for you', 'for your family') contain a personal noun group denoting potential beneficiaries. Although this unusual minor clause construction is apparently more frequent in television than in press advertising, it may have come into use through two-part display headings such as:

> For the cat who knows what's best for him
>
> JELLYMEAT WHISKAS

where the brand-name, in large type, is joined with a less prominently printed catch phrase. In this case, the difference between the A Z structure and the Z A structure ('Manns for happy Christmas time') would have originally been simply a matter of lay-out: whether the main heading was placed above or below the accompanying slogan.

The identification of clauses with the structure Z A is problematic because of the overlap between what can operate as an adjunct in clause structure and as a post-modifer in nominal group structure. In the Lifeguard example quoted above, the solution lies in the incompatibility in group structure of a head such as 'Lifeguard' with an embedded modifier such as 'in your home'. (True, a clause such as 'Lifeguard in your home is the answer to your problems', in which this construction acts as subject, is a possibility. But in this case too, it would be regarded as a minor clause: an embedded clause as subject parallel to the non-finite clause 'Using Lifeguard' in 'Using Lifeguard is the answer to your problems'. This would be indicated by the necessity of having an abstract noun group such as 'the answer to your problems' as complement.)

'When', 'If', and 'Because'

Dependent clauses beginning with *when*, *if* and *because* have special functions in advertising copy.

When, as it is most commonly used, joins a clause about the product to a clause about the consumer's needs and their satisfaction. It is not a temporal so much as a conditional conjunction, equivalent to *whenever*. In the following examples, the whole sentence formed by the two clauses amounts to a claim 'whenever product X is used, Y is the result':

> You'll wonder where the yellow went
> When you brush your teeth with Pepsodent.

> When you take an instant Daxaid, you feel it disperse on your tongue.

> And when you Snowcem you'll see the improvement miles away!

Alternatively, the independent clause is the clause about the product, and a preceding clause states the condition:

> When you have an orange, have a Jaffa!
> When you need aspirin, drink Disprin!

These two sentences exemplify a characteristic combination of a *when* clause with an imperative clause. *You* is almost invariably the subject of a *when* clause.

The tendency for the dependent clause to precede the independent one is strong in the case of *when* clauses, and even stronger for *if* clauses, which are regressive almost without exception, even when complex:

> If you're a wife who believes that the best Home-made Bread is made with good honest plain flour – then this flour, made by McDougall's, is the flour for you . . .

> . . . but if by mid-week the shelves are getting bare, and money's short, then six extra eggs will make a really good meal . . .

It was pointed out earlier (p. 107) that the main advertising function of *if* clauses is to single out the right category of consumer. But this often happens to be a rather comprehensive class of people. In the first of these two examples, the evaluative loading of the *if* clause ('good honest plain flour') suggests that no self-respecting housewife ought to consider herself excluded. The right category of consumer in the following case is even wider; it embraces the whole of mankind, jelly-addicts and non-jelly-addicts:

> If you're a jelly-addict
> Or even if you aren't
> You'll find that Chivers' satisfy
> Like other jellies can't.

Placing the *if* clause in front of the clause on which it depends seems the most forceful and natural way of expressing this kind of condition, particularly in advertising, where the *if* clause makes an initial bid for attention by appealing to the consumer's interest in herself. But on the other hand, this can lead, as we have seen, to considerable complexity of anticipatory structure, and it is not surprising that use is made of an alternative mode of expression, where a *Yes/No* question is used in place of the *if* clause. The sentence

> If you suffer from indigestion, this is something you'll want to know

could have been replaced by two sentences with the same meaning and effect:

> Suffer from indigestion? This is something you'll want to know.

This is the alternative preferred in another health advertisement:

> Running a temperature? Feeling low? Look after him well – and give him the goodness of Lucozade.

Both these means of expressing a condition are favourite openings for medicine advertisements, where the first task of the copywriter is to seek the ear of sufferers from the particular ailment his product claims to relieve.

In my television sample, the *because* clause contrasted strongly with the *if* clause, in that it invariably followed the main clause:

> Now Johnson's Glo-Coat becomes *Super* Glo-Coat – because the new formula is three ways better.

In addition, it was often separated from the preceding main clause by a phonological break indicating the greatest degree of finality: a tone-group boundary preceded by a falling tone and marked by a pause. These two factors together suggest that at least in spoken advertising the word *because* is more like a conjunctive adverb (*so, therefore, yet,* etc.) than a subordinating conjunction: it can plausibly be treated as the beginning of a new sentence. This analysis would not apply to press advertising, where anticipatory *because* clauses are occasionally found in detailed explanatory copy. Another significant feature of the television sample was the absence from direct address copy of clauses of reason introduced by *as* or *since*; these probably have a more formal stylistic range than *because* clauses.

The chief role of a *because* clause is, obviously enough, to give a reason for buying the product. For example, in the commercial from which the above sentence was quoted, the copy goes on to expand 'three ways better' by enumerating three improvements to the product. This is copy of the 'logical' or 'reason why' type; but it should not be assumed that *because* is always associated with a practical justification of the selling promise. 'A because B' is not a rational argument, in an acceptable understanding of the term 'rational', unless the assertion B has some material or factual foundation. This can scarcely be claimed for such a sentence as:

> Make *sure* it's Cadbury's. Because no other chocolate can possibly give you the proper, creamy, Cadbury taste.

We might ask, in view of the positional restriction of the *because* clause, what happens when the copywriter wants to state the reason before the conclusion: 'B therefore A'. *Therefore* is far too formal a connective, but the conjunctive adverb *so* and the formula 'That's why . . .' are acceptably colloquial alternatives:

Men love cheese. So next time you pack his lunchbox pop in some cheese and an apple.

Good tobacco and a good tip give you better taste and more of it. That's why there's no mistaking the Nelson touch.

When there's a baby in the house, cleanness matters so much more. That's why so many mothers are using Clinic Shampoo.

Both these are much used in advertising language.

Chapter 13

Verbal Groups

Above the rank of group, there is remarkably little grammatical complexity in advertising English. The following details emerged from the study of the television sample:

1. More than three out of four clauses were independent. By far the majority of sentences, then, contained no dependence structure.

2. One in five independent clauses was a minor clause. As minor clauses usually contained only one element (z or A), this amounted to a large proportion of maximally simple clauses.

3. Over one in four major independent clauses was an imperative clause. Imperative clauses have no subject, so this again contributed to overall simplicity of clauses.

4. There was less than one adjunct per clause.

Press copy, it is true, is a little more complex than television copy in these respects; but not enough to affect the validity of my opening observation.

At the rank of group, however, there is a significant disparity in complexity in different classes of group. Nominal groups, at least in pre-modification, are often complex. But verbal groups are mostly of maximum simplicity, consisting of only one word. Complexity in the nominal group, simplicity elsewhere: this is a generalisation which can be confirmed by grammatical analysis of practically any piece of advertising copy. If on first impression an advertisement appears to be linguistically complex, further investigation usually shows that complexity is limited to nominal group structure. Here is an extreme instance of this tendency:

Headline: Holiday Colour Snaps!

Subhead: Save up to 23/3 with half-price processing from Film Exchange

Body copy: Through **Film Exchange**, direct-from-laboratory-processing achieves sensational savings for amateur colour photographers. **Finest quality colour processing** of these internationally famous films – **at half cost**! Order the film of your choice (at normal retail price) from the list below, and you qualify for the **special Film Exchange all-in processing rates which include a reload film with your results.**

The only words which do not belong to nominal group structure here (either directly or through embedding) are a handful of prepositions, verbs and conjunctions: *save, up, to, with, from,* etc. Among the more complex, heavily modified nominals groups are:

amateur colour photographers
finest quality colour processing
these internationally famous films
the special Film Exchange all-in processing rates which include a
   reload film with your results

All verbal groups, on the other hand, consist of single words: *save, achieves, order, qualify, include.* In this and the following chapter we shall explore this contrast between the two group classes, and seek possible explanations for it.

Simplicity in the Verbal Group

For a discussion of simplicity in the verbal group, we shall limit our attention to the finite verbal group, which may consist of single-word present tense, past tense, or imperative forms (*gives, gave, give*) or of a sequence of two, three, four, or even more words: 'will give', 'has given', 'is being given', 'will have been given', and so on. Twenty-four secondary classes of the verbal group are derived by simultaneous selection from the following systems:

TENSE		ASPECT (1)	
Present	*gives*	Non-perfective	*gives*
Past	*gave*	Perfective	*has given*
Future	*will give*		

ASPECT (2)		VOICE	
Non-durative	*gives*	Active	*gives*
Durative	*is giving*	Passive	*is given*

Selection of the first term in each of these systems yields the single-word present form *gives.* If on the other hand, each of the last terms are selected, the result is a rather improbably complex (but nevertheless occurring) class of group: 'will have been being given'. The first term in the last three systems can be considered a 'neutral' term, which is marked by no special grammatical form, and is defined simply as the negation of the second, or 'marked' term. By selecting a combination of marked and unmarked terms we arrive at groups such as 'is giving' (present durative) and 'has been given' (present perfective passive). To simplify the names of these classes, the choice of an unmarked term (non-perfective, non-durative, active) is assumed if its contrary is not specified.

It is no doubt generally true of the English verbal group that complexity of structure correlated with infrequency of occurrence. But in advertising English the preference for unmarked terms is particularly prominent. This can be checked by a random glance through the advertising material quoted in this book: by far the majority of finite verbal groups are either simple present forms (*gives*, etc.) or else simple imperatives. Less impressionistically, it is confirmed by a comparison of verbal groups in direct address copy and in indirect address copy, under the assumption that the former reflects the specialisation of the advertising role more than the latter. In the television sample, spoken commentary contained over twice the proportion of non-perfective to perfective forms found in monologue and dialogue; and the disparity was almost as marked in the preference of non-durative to durative forms. In passive groups, the inequality was more striking in indirect address copy, mainly because of the special role of locutions such as '. . . is made by . . .' in direct address advertising (see p. 82). However, there is independent evidence of the infrequency of passive groups in advertising copy, in comparison with other varieties of English.*

The preference of present tense to past tense groups, though not a matter of structural complexity, was also much greater in commentary than in indirect address situations. There was approximately one past tense form to every six present tense forms in indirect address compared with only one to twenty in commentary. The avoidance of the past tense in direct address has some connection with the infrequency of perfective and durative forms, in that the present tense might on *semantic* grounds (but not on formal grounds) be considered the unmarked term of the tense system. So by this view (to be elaborated shortly) the past tense would be a marked term, and the generalisation could be made that in

---

* In Chapter 7 of his study, *On Voice in the English Verb* (The Hague, 1966), Jan Svartvik shows that television advertising is second only to comic dramatic dialogue in the rarity of the passive voice; the dialogue of novels and even natural speech itself use the passive considerably more frequently.

every system the copywriter shows a strong preference for unmarked terms.

Tense and Aspect

What is the significance of the outstanding frequency of simple present forms of advertising? The label 'present' is semantically misleading in so far as it suggests an *exclusion* of past and future time. The simple present has two very different meanings, which may be distinguished as the INSTANTANEOUS PRESENT and the UNRESTRICTIVE PRESENT. The difference between them is schematically represented in this diagram which translates the time dimension into left-to-right sequence in space:

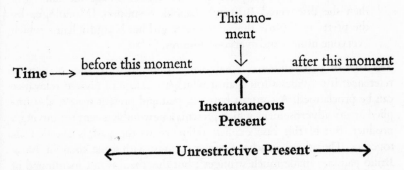

The instantaneous present does indeed have the meaning 'exclusion of past and future time': it is used for the description of an event begun and completed at the very moment of speech. But besides being limited to verbs which can refer to momentary events (*put, hit, fall*, etc., but not *live, stay, run*, etc.), it is rarely used outside expressions describing the perceptual or mental reactions of speaker and audience: 'I see'; 'Do you give up?'; 'You amaze me'; etc. The unrestrictive present, the most important use of this verb form, refers to a time period which includes the present moment, and also stretches indefinitely into the past and future, unless limitation is implied by other forms (for example, by the time adverb *nowadays* in 'Nowadays he smokes a pipe').

Advertising English happens to be one of the registers of English in which the instantaneous present is used outside the limiting conditions just mentioned. 'Now I *try* and wash off the ink with water' is an example of its use in demonstration commercials, to describe an action simultaneously shown on the screen. In 'Down *goes* the price of Sainsbury's chicken', the instantaneous present is used with dramatic licence, to heighten the spectacular nature of the event. But the vast majority of present tense forms are the unrestrictive type: 'Milk – the drink that *helps* us to make the most of our leisure'; 'You *get* twice as much goodness with Campbell's Soup'. This is clearly in line with the copywriter's interest in making his claims as absolute as possible. One might say that for advertising purposes, the virtues of the product are for all time, like the laws of nature.

We may now look at some negative aspects of this choice: the reasons for avoiding the past, durative and perfective classes of the verbal group.

The past tense has a place in advertising language whenever a contrast has to be made between 'now' and 'then'. This usually means a consumer's history before and after using the product:

> Once upon a time this pretty girl had dry unmanageable hair – But then she discovered Bristow's Lanolin Shampoo. [Monologue by the pretty girl] Now this same pretty girl has beautiful hair – which everyone notices and everyone admires.

The role of past reference is habitually subordinate to that of present reference: it provides a foil against which a message of present relevance can be proclaimed. A contrast between past and present time is also implied in any advertisement which presents a new inducement for buying a product. But in this case explicit reference to the past is avoided altogether. The adverb *now* has a covert contrast with some 'then' in 'Now Brillo pads are made much stronger'; but the 'then' is not mentioned in the advertisement. We would obviously not expect a semantically equivalent sentence which placed emphasis on the product prior to improvement: 'Once Brillo pads were made much weaker'.

The key to the infrequency of the past tense is its exclusion of reference to the present moment, which is the central point of orientation for any advertising message. The durative aspect has a limitation of a different kind. It may be selected with the present tense (as in 'is giving') and is therefore compatible with present reference, but in its most important sense, it applies only to *temporary* activity. The different effects of the simple present and the present durative can be tested if 'are settling' is substituted for 'settle' in the sentence: 'Every day more smokers settle for the Nelson touch'. As it stands, this seems to state a general law: the consumption of Nelson cigarettes has increased, is increasing, and will continue to increase. But 'Every day more smokers are settling for the Nelson touch' would describe a movement which happens to be in progress at the present time. The greater immediacy of the durative aspect may be valuable when the fashionable appeal of the product is under emphasis: 'This is the smoke that's *setting* the trend'. However, this advantage is usually outweighed by the greater generality of the non-durative form.

As the perfective aspect mostly refers, like the past tense, to antecedent states and events, its utility in consumer advertising is limited in the same way. Both classes, however, are common in prestige advertising, where they are used to report the history and achievements of the advertising firm.

'Will' and 'Can'

So far no comment has been made on the future tense. The future auxiliary *will* (or more frequently the contraction *'ll*) is one exception to the general infrequency of auxiliary verbs in advertising language. The other exception is the modal auxiliary *can*. The relevance of these items to advertising can be summed up in the words 'promise' and 'opportunity'.

It could be claimed that all consumer advertisments express a promise of the underlying form 'If you buy X, Y will be the result'. Advertising copy rarely contains actual sentences of this kind, because preference is given to sentences of equivalent effect, in which an imperative clause performs the function of the conditional clause: 'Put out Swoop, and the birds will soon come'. The future tense occurs in the second clause, which expresses the promise. It also often occurs in sentences like 'This free booklet will tell you more about it' or 'You'll love Carnation Caramel Custard', where the condition is unexpressed. It seemed to be assumed that the addressee is going to buy the product. But perhaps in some of these cases, the future expresses not so much futurity as the infallibility of the claim. Under this interpretation, a slightly stronger paraphrase of 'You'll love Carnation Caramel Custard' would be 'You cannot help but like Carnation Caramel Custard'. (Compare the use of *will* in aphorisms like 'Boys will be boys' and 'Accidents will happen'.)

Can has one of two meanings in advertising copy, depending on whether it is preceded by an animate or inanimate subject. The animate subject is most often *you* (i.e. the consumer): '*You can* wash the big city right out of your hair'; 'Find out about the cheapest central heating *you can* buy'. In these sentences, the consumer is told that the product gives her the *power* or *ability* to do this or that. An inanimate subject will most often be either the brand-name itself or a noun referentially connected with the product: 'Rogor can save you up to £5 an acre'; 'Yes, Beecham's Pills can bring the health that means more than wealth'. Here the vision of opportunity is seen from the opposite angle: the consumer is told what *possibilities* the product offers for satisfying his needs or otherwise benefiting him.

Chapter 14
Nominal Groups

The category 'nominal group', as used in this description, is a broad class including structures which have nouns, pronouns, adjectives, determiners, or numerals as their primary (i.e. obligatory) elements. However, the most important and potentially complex secondary structure is that of the noun group – the group which has a noun as its head. In advertising language, the interesting part of the noun group is the pre-modifying part, which is sometimes marked not only by outstanding complexity, but by certain unusual features of structure.

Technical Pre-modifiers

At the beginning of Chapter 13, I gave an illustration of the complexity noun groups can attain in advertising copy which has to go into a technical description of the product or service offered. Here is a further example, in which noun groups with lengthy pre-modifications are italicised:

> Fantastic acceleration from *the 95 b.h.p. Coventry Climax O.H.C. engine*, more stopping power from the *new 4-wheel servo assisted disc brakes* and greater flexibility from *the all synchromesh close ratio gearbox*. These and many other new refinements combine to present *the finest and fastest light G.T. car in the world*.

In complex noun groups such as these, much of the pre-modification serves to specify in detail what the product is like, and how it works. They follow a trend which has been noted in modern English generally, and particularly in the English of technological communication. Randolph Quirk in *The Use of English**★** quotes a particularly astonishing example of noun group pre-modification from an iron and steel company's public notice: 'the redesign and enlargement of *the Company's eight fixed open hearth steel melting furnaces*'. Critics of this tendency in technical writing

---

★ Quirk (1962), pp. 161 and 164.

might, as Quirk points out, favour something like 'eight furnaces, of a fixed type with open hearth, for the melting of steel'. The 'translation' of pre-modifiers into post-modifiers might make the meaning more explicit, but would certainly make for an intolerably cumbersome style of expression. I would also claim that the two expressions are semantically different: whereas the noun with pre-modification denotes a specific category of furnace, the same noun with equivalent post-modification describes furnaces with certain attributes in common. This rather subtle distinction is analogous to that between 'black birds' and 'blackbirds', where this time it is the structure with pre-modification, as opposed to the compound noun, which illustrates the attributive function. Pre-modifiers which can have the designative, or categorising function are nouns, adjectives and compounds. Adjectives are most commonly used in this way in scientific English (for example, *hydrochloric* in 'hydrochloric acid' labels a certain category of chemical substance); an example in advertising language is *decorative* in 'Natural Teak and Antique Soft-glow Formica decorative laminate'. In this group (itself an outstanding instance of piled up pre-modification), *decorative* does not have the usual sense 'pleasing to look at': instead, it helps to specify more exactly the kind of material referred to as 'laminate'. The class of designative adjectives is probably identical with that of 'non-gradable' adjectives, i.e. those which cannot be preceded by sub-modifiers such as *very*, *quite*, and *slightly*.

English has a limited number of common nouns; but through compounding and pre-modification, it has the means of extending the 'labelling' function of language to an indefinitely large number of objects.* This helps to explain why in technical and scientific English these aspects of noun group structure are exploited to a greater extent than elsewhere.

The type of advertising copy which contains technical or semi-technical information is mainly found in press advertising. The example at the beginning of this chapter was taken from a magazine of specialised readership, *The Motor*: this is the sort of publication in which technical language is in any case found in articles and features. On television, there is not the time to go into detail on the technicalities of a product, and even if there were, the audience would probably fail to take in the details on the single hearing. Technical copy requires a public which is interested, and has the leisure to take careful note of the information given in the advertisement.

---

* Cf. Lees (1960), pp. xvii–xviii.

Attributive Pre-modifiers

If one reason for complexity of pre-modification is to give information about the product, another equally important one is that of giving glowingly attractive descriptions of it. This is the province of attributive, rather than of designative adjectives. Some attributive adjectives, such as *good*, *lovely*, and *excellent* are purely evaluative in meaning; others have strong overtones of value-judgement, which in the context of advertising naturally means approbation rather than disapprobation. The cumulative evocative effect of adjectives in advertising copy can be seen in the following extracts:

> Noisily crisp celery. Lettuce green and toothsome. Cool, thirst-quenching cucumber. Taste-tempting tomatoes.

> They go for its fresh, wake-up tang, its thick satisfying texture.

In such purple passages, an alluring picture is painted not only by piling up regular attributive adjectives (*crisp*, *green*, *cool*, etc.) but by coining vividly descriptive compounds and using unusually expressive sub-modifiers like *noisily*, *appetisingly*, *mouthwateringly*. But here we will consider only the adjectives. Clusters of two adjectives are common in all advertising (for some reason, particularly so in television jingles), and clusters of three adjectives are not unusual: 'Such deep, rich, springy pile'; 'Golden, bubbling, toasted cheese'.

Two kinds of adjective clusters have an emphatically emotive effect. The first is formed by a repetition of the same adjective: 'Wonderful, wonderful Roses'; 'a big big bottle'. The second, which is especially common in advertising, consists of an approbatory adjective followed by one or more concrete meaning: 'this wonderful new toothbrush'; 'lovely rich fruit cakes'. Both these types belong to colloquial English, and are perhaps associated more than anything with the language used by grown-ups in addressing children. They are basically means of emotive intensification. The repetition of *big* in 'a big big bottle' does not add denotative meaning: it simply adds emphasis. Likewise, the first adjective of 'lovely rich fruit cakes' tells us less about the cakes than about the speaker's attitude.

Commendation and Information Together

The most distinctive type of complex noun group in advertising is that which contains pre-modifiers of both the attributive and designative kind:

Elegant tapered slacks – Rugged Western style Jeans – Matching two-tone Jeans/Shirt sets – Snappy ankle flared beat Jeans and a wide choice of colour, pattern and texture.

In this list of merchandise, each noun group begins with two adjectival elements. In three of the four groups, the first adjective is chiefly evaluative in import (*elegant, rugged, snappy*), whereas the second element (compound or adjective) specifies the class of garment more exactly. Some further examples of combined attributive and designative pre-modification are: 'Its natural germ-killing action'; 'these attractive matching cases'; 'a really first-rate imported sherry'; 'Four smart two-tone colour schemes'. It is not surprising that the copywriter should mingle praise with practicality. He usually needs to include both in his message, and the more closely interwoven they are, the better. It is not his aim to help the public, as some newspapers do, by a rigid separation of fact and opinion.

Product Names

The extreme frequency of references to the advertised product provides another reason for heavy pre-modification in the noun group. Products can, of course, be referred to quite simply by the mention of a brand-name such as *Eno* or *Maxwell House*, or by using the manufacturer's trade name as a means of identification: *Addis, Campbell's, Players*. A slightly more lengthy means of referring to a product is a combination of the advertiser's name or brand-name with a word or phrase designating the product: 'Campbell's Soup'; 'Fray Bentos Steak and Kidney Pie'. Further complexity arises when all three are included: 'Kraft Superfine Margarine'; 'Carling's Black Label Canadian Lager'. From these examples, it can be seen that quite a long string of words can be used to label a product – a tendency which is extreme in an example quoted earlier in the chapter: 'Natural Teak and Antique Softglow Formica decorative laminate'.

All these designative expressions, whether they consist of one word or several, may be termed 'product names'. On packages and labels, a fairly full type of product name usually appears, with the brand-name set off the rest by extra large lettering. In advertisements, a product is often referred to by designations of varying length. In one commercial, for example, the product was called in turn 'Carling's Black Label Canadian Lager', 'Carling's Black Label', and 'Carling's Lager Beer'.

In cases like this the brand-name and other elements of the product name show a readiness to shift their syntactic function. In 'Carling's Black Label Canadian Lager', the brand-name 'Black Label' is a compound pre-modifier; in 'Black Label' it is itself a whole noun group with the structure E H (see p. 14 for the function of the symbols D, O, E, N, and H in the description of the nominal group). The noun *lager* similarly alters its status from noun modifier to head in 'Carling's Lager Beer' and 'Carling's Black Label Canadian Lager'. In general, there are signs that brand-names have an unstable syntactic function. They may act as N modifiers even when they stand alone in the group: in 'Corona are the finest drinks', *Corona* is marked as N, not H, by the lack of number agreement with the verb. But in other cases, the brand-name operates as head, inflecting for singular and plural: someone at a tobacconist's shop might ask for 'twenty Oliviers' (O H) or 'twenty Olivier' (O N).

There are one or two other syntactic oddities associated with the use of brand-names and product names. 'Carling Black Label Canadian Lager' illustrates how a brand-name, which I suppose should be classified as an N modifier, sometimes precedes an adjective which is part of the product name. This is a disruption of the normal order of elements (E N) in nominal group structure. More generally, a brand-name tends to be placed in an early position in a noun group, whether the noun group designates a product, or some feature associated with a product: 'Swoop balanced-formula wild bird food'; 'the Austin A 55 sports car gear lever'; 'Alka-Seltzer all-over action.'

A product name sometimes contains adjectives of an attributive character: 'Liquid *Bubbly* Stergene'. In this case, further pre-modifications may violate the general rule that attributive pre-modifiers precede designative ones. *Liquid* in this example is marginally designative; and the further designative epithets *new-label* and *improved* in 'new-label improved Bubbly Stergene' certainly appear in an abnormally early position. The explanation of this peculiarity is that a product name like other proper names (e.g. 'St. Paul's Cathedral'; 'the Board of Trade') acts as a single syntactic 'block' analogous in many ways to a single noun; however, unlike other names, its structural composition may change, and may include attributive elements.

This brings us to another notable feature of noun groups containing product names. Proper names usually admit of a very limited amount of extraneous modification. Semantically, this is easy to understand. Modifiers, as the name suggests, generally have the function of restricting the range of denotata referred to by the head. This is true of both designative and attributive modifiers: 'apple pie' has more specific reference than 'pie', and 'red hair' than 'hair'. It is this property that semantically dis-tinuishes restrictive (embedded) relative clauses ('Children *whom he loved* often visited him') from non-restrictive ones, which in writing are set off from their antecedents by punctuation: 'Children, *whom he loved*, often visited him'. As proper names have unique reference, and so cannot be more specific than they are, it would appear that restrictive modifiers cannot be meaningfully attached to them. In fact they can be, but only when there is *ambiguity* of reference ('Jeannie with the light brown hair' carries the implication '. . . as opposed to any girl of that name with hair of a different hue'); or when there is a figurative pluralisation of the re-ferent ('the America I loved' implies '. . . as opposed to other Americas you or I might know of'). In such cases, the proper noun seems to be temporarily transferred to the category of common nouns.

On the other hand, proper nouns do occasionally combine with modi-fiers of non-restrictive force: 'fair Helen' (= 'Helen, who is fair', not 'the Helen who is fair'); 'beautiful Britain'; 'poor John'. This type of pre-modifier, which is mainly confined to items of emotive or evaluative import, commonly precedes product names in advertising: 'crisp, tasty, whole wheat Cubs'; 'new and chewy G.B. Mints'. The listing of two or more non-restrictive adjective modifiers, as in these examples, is almost exclusively a characteristic of advertising English. Even more unusual are post-modifying phrases used in the same way: 'Gibbs S.R. with the new – active – tingle'; 'Rowntree's Fruit Pastilles with the tingle-tongue taste'; 'Du Maurier Virginia cigarettes of exceptional quality'.

It might be objected that product names are not true proper names, be-cause on occasion they can be used in a generic sense, as in 'I'm getting a new Austin'; 'Can I borrow your Ajax?'. But this interpretation clearly does not fit the cited cases. It is hardly likely that the writer of 'new and chewy G.B. Mints' meant 'the G.B. Mints which are new and chewy (as opposed to those which are old and hard on the teeth)'. The product name is intended as a proper name, and is understood as such.

The use of non-restrictive modifiers with product names relates to the use of attributive epithets *within* product names. They are both desig-natively redundant, and contribute only to the evaluative aspect of the advertising message, by building up favourable associations with the product.

Some Classes of Modifier

Having noted some general reasons for complexity of pre-modification in noun groups, we will examine the special functions of some modifying classes not included in previous discussion: genitives, comparative and superlative adjectives, and noun modifiers.

Genitives in English are largely limited to animate, if not personal noun groups; genitives like 'Charlie's' and 'my friend's' are common, 'the book's' and 'democracy's' less so. However, in advertising language a significantly large proportion of genitives do not belong to the animate category. It is true that the most numerous type of genitive is one that has a manufacturer's name, which can be construed as an animate noun, as its stem: 'Campbell's Soup'; 'Bristow's special Lanolin'. But three other prominent types do not have this grammatical property: 'And pineapple needs *Carnation's* creamy goodness, too'; '. . . post the coupon from *this week's* T.V. Times'; 'Win *Britain's* most exciting family car'. These three examples illustrate respectively the genitival use of brand-names, nouns of time, and nouns of place. In 'Kellogg's Rice Krispies great new card series', a whole product name 'Kellogg's Rice Krispies' is used genitively, itself containing a further genitive ('Kellogg's'). (That 'Kellogg's Rice Krispies' is a genitive rather than a plural N modifier, in spite of the omission of a concluding apostrophe, is shown by the absence of a definite or indefinite article at the beginning of the group.) Genitives of time ('to-day's', 'this week's', etc.) are not uncommon in modern English, but their use seems especially characteristic of public-colloquial registers – above all, popular journalism and advertising. Both these and genitives of place commonly precede superlative adjectives, or other modifiers of absolute meaning: 'this year's *most wanted* refrigerator'; 'the world's *leading* laminate'.

The frequent use of comparative and superlative adjectives is such an obvious trait of advertising language that little need be said about it. These classes of adjective are common both in noun groups ('You'll have *fresher* breath, *healthier* teeth and *whiter* teeth'; 'the *finest* beans that ever grew'); and in adjective groups ('It's *better* than the average cereal'; '. . . because it's the *best*'). *Better* and *best* are especially common; occurrences of the latter made up almost a third of all superlatives in the television sample. Other items are mostly of the kind expressing some desirable quality: *finest, greater, softer*, etc.

Modifying nouns apart from brand-names are mainly associated with the designative semantic function, and therefore with the informative, rather than associative aspect of advertising language. As a class, the noun modifier has a semantic relation to its head which is multiply ambiguous to the point of vagueness, although in individual cases the meaning is clear, so that it is possible to give a more explicit paraphrase through post-modification: 'garden birds' = 'birds which frequent gardens'; 'Sunday paper' = 'paper published on Sundays'; 'town living' = 'living in towns'; 'foil wrapping' = 'wrapping made of foil'. The potential vagueness of this construction allows copywriters to use it occasionally for emotive, as well as informative purposes: 'the full, natural *sunshine flavour* of tree-fresh Australian fruit'. In an unusual collocation of items such as this, there is no easily defined semantic relationship between the nouns. We might be able to supply a rather far-fetched paraphrase such as 'flavour which results from exposure to sunshine'. But the point of the collocation is rather in the emotive associations of the word *sunshine*, just as in another example, 'summer freshness', *summer* contributes favourable connotations to the meaning of *freshness*. A tendency to exercise licence in the collocation of noun with noun is also observable in a favourite advertising construction in which *way* is preceded by an N modifier: 'Nylon stays gay the *Stergene way*'; 'the *film-star way* to a softer, more radiant complexion'.

Chapter 15

Words and Compounds

Perhaps the most conspicuous characteristic of advertising language to a casual reader or listener is an abundance and variety of adjectival compounds. Quite a number have been seen in the last chapter, and anyone can soon find further examples by looking through the advertising pages of a few newspapers and magazines. In turning to this subject, we shall be merely continuing the theme of Chapter 14, by considering complexity of pre-modification in embedded structure instead of place-ordered structure. However, this begs a question which has vexed grammarians through the ages, and to which I must now attempt an answer.

What is a Compound?

First of all, as suggested in the linguistic introduction, any definition of the compound, or for that matter any other grammatical category, based on orthography has to be rejected. 'A compound is a sequence of two or more words not separated by a space in writing': this is unworkable both because it does not help with spoken language, and because orthographic practice in the use of hyphens and spaces is notoriously inconsistent. Grammatical problems require grammatical solutions, and in the present context, this means that a compound is to be defined by reference to units and structures in English grammar.

There is a latent element of paradox in our common understanding of the word 'compound'; a compound is somehow conceived of as a 'group of words' which is nevertheless a 'single word'. These contradictory notions can be reconciled through the concept of embedding. If a compound is considered a group or clause embedded within group structure, this is tantamount to saying that it is a sequence of words *acting* as a single word. Thus in 'sophisticated, sweet-to-drink Pink Lady', *sweet-to-drink* is a sequence of words (in fact an adjective group) operating as a single pre-modifier, in a position which makes it equivalent to an adjective. This explanation will not cover all cases, as some structures we recognise as compounds are *words* with embedded structure. *Hard-hearted*, for example, may be analysed as an adjective (parallel in structure to *wooded*, *carpeted*, etc.) which has 'hard heart', an embedded noun group with the structure E H, as its stem.

However, even this characterisation is not complete, because it does not accommodate the *lexical* aspect of compounding. Compounds are generally single items of vocabulary, which have to be individually listed in a dictionary. This is another reason why compounds have been considered words; for the word, as a grammatical unit, is typically coextensive with the lexical item.

What is involved in the statement that as a rule compounds, like words, 'have to be listed in a dictionary'? Grammatical structures above word rank are normally fully productive, in the sense that their acceptability is fully determined by the rules of grammar. But morphology is a different matter. A rule can be stated whereby the suffix *-ful* is added to abstract nouns to form adjectives like *beautiful*, *hateful*, *slothful*, etc. But it does not extend to all noun stems of the same grammatical class: if it did, it would permit the construction of un-English adjectives such as *loveful*, *stealthful*, and *greedful*. This rule is only partially productive, and its domain has to be circumscribed by listing those forms to which it does apply. In this we see how lexical statements, in so far as they are concerned with cataloguing the language's vocabulary, imply special restrictions on the generality of grammatical statements.

Lexical 'productiveness' is a relative matter, extending from fully unproductive affixes such as the *-th* of *stealth*, *width*, *depth*, etc. to fully productive patterns in the higher grammatical ranks. Some types of compound such as the noun + noun type of *schoolboy* are near to fully productive, whereas others, such as the type represented by *Englishman*, are not. Perhaps if any formal significance can be attached to the various orthographic ways of representing a compound (as two or more words, as one hyphenated word, or as a single undivided word), they are indications of the extent to which the compound is felt to be an established item of vocabulary. Thus *air craft*, *air-craft*, and *aircraft* might represent three stages on the path to full lexical acceptance.

The Compounding Propensity in Advertising

I have suggested here that a compound be regarded as a lexically restricted unit containing embedded structure. We must now consider how this reflects on the profusion of *ad hoc* compounds in advertising English.

This phenomenon could be considered a repeated violation of lexical restraints, indicating individual copywriters' whimsical love of linguistic invention. But it is clearly not a matter of individual copywriting styles, but of the advertising register as a whole. So a better way to explain it is to say that *in advertising English, lexical restraints on compound formation are less stringent than elsewhere*. To clarify this, let us imagine a variety of English in which lexical restrictions on compound formation are completely relaxed, at least in respect of compound modifiers:

> Poor-neighbourhood Charles was not, as one might have supposed, the most-difficulty-causing child. Although he was learning-slow and loss-of-interest-inclined, he would sit for hours mouse-quiet and lamb-docile when constructive-task-involved. But parent-doted-on, every-whim-indulged Paul sought all-through-the-day attention, often throwing middle-of-the-classroom annoy-the-teacher tantrums.

Whereas advertising English is a long way from this hypothetical extreme, something of the range of tolerated compounding in pre-modification can be seen in this press advertisement. (Compounds are italicised.)

Headline: Peerless brings within your reach . . . the luxury of a *Built-in-Bedroom* at a price you can really afford With *Dovetail Self-assembly* Units

Body copy: The marvellous new Peerless *Dovetail* idea brings you the bedroom you've longed for at an *undreamed-of* saving.
This *craftsman-made* furniture is delivered straight from the factory to your home . . . a big saving to begin with! It is ready for quick and effortless '*slot-together*' assembly – you can complete a roomful in a day.
There is a full range of different units to fit any room and they can be ordered separately. Wardrobes start from as little as £9 3.6.
Surround yourself with luxury in the Peerless tradition . . . contemporary in styling, *space-saving* in design, and so elegant in appearance. Peerless Dovetail units use only *Highest Quality* Materials and are fully guaranteed. Top surfaces are 'Formica'.

Some shorter extracts will illustrate the more exotic style of compounding in press copy: 'Junior Couture Lingerie (and *safer-from-fire* Sleepwear) by Judy'; 'The "*so many ways*" cheese'; 'Veet "O" leaves skin *satin-soft*, makes *underarms* immaculate, arms and legs *fuzz-free*'; 'Lifebuoy Toilet Soap with Puralin gives *day in-day out* protection against B.O.'.

Compound Pre-modifiers

The two most important types of compound in English are those which operate respectively as pre-modifier and as head within the nominal group. The former type includes ADJECTIVAL COMPOUNDS which operate at E in group structure. In the following classified list, each structural category of adjectival compound is introduced with a familiar compound which illustrates the pattern. Many of the examples, however, will be 'nonce compounds' demonstrating the productive use of the pattern. All compounds are hyphenated, for the sake of consistency.

FIRST-CLASS. 'these twenty *top-quality* bulbs'; 'the *economy-size* Shredded Wheat'. (This type has a noun of measure or value as its second element.)

BRAND-NEW. 'the *farmhouse-fresh* taste'; '*feather-light* flakes'; '*sugar-crisp* bubbles of wheat'; '. . . to keep you looking *band-box-smart*'.

ICY-COLD. '*creamy-mild* Lux Soap'; 'a fabulous *deep-cold* freezer'; 'That's Mary Baker's Sweet-Bake – *crusty-gold, saucy-good* . . .'.

PIPING-HOT. '*shining-clean* pans'; 'Your paintwork comes up *sparkling-clean* . . .'.

HOME-MADE. '*honey-coated* Sugar Puffs'; 'an attractive *mink-toned* case'; 'the only *chocolate-flavoured* cereal'.

HARD-HEARTED. 'a *stiff-tufted* mud remover'; '*perfect-textured* cakes'; 'the *full-flavoured* fruit juice'.

RECORD-BREAKING. 'the unbreakable *hand-fitting* container'; 'a *relief-giving* liquid'; 'these extra *home-making* booklets'; 'Newsome cloth is *rain-and-stain-resisting*'.

GOOD-LOOKING. 'the *best-looking* small car in the world'; '*good-tasting* oats and wheat Trios'; 'this *different-tasting* Sparkling Tango'.

HARD-WORKING. '*fast-foaming* new S.R.'; 'the *best-selling* soft toilet tissue'; 'That's the Remington shave – closer, smoother, *longer-lasting*'.

Of particular interest are compounds which themselves contain a compound as one of their elements: *farmhouse-fresh*; *coffee-pot-fresh*; *brand-*

new-clean. *Coffee-pot-fresh* belongs to the pattern 'brand-new', except that a noun compound, instead of a simple noun, fills the first position. Similarly, *Brand-new-clean* is like *icy-cold*.

In addition to adjectival compounds, there are types of pre-modifying compounds whose exact status within the nominal group is uncertain. Their occurrence is limited to noun groups, and I have found no evidence for deciding to which of the two elements E or N they should be assigned. They include:

EMBEDDED NOUN GROUPS. '*high-fashion* knitwear'; 'its wonderful *fresh-milk* taste'; '*fuller-flavour* fishsteaks'; 'their *fine-powder* form'; '*whole-house* heating'; 'the *all-purpose* garden fertiliser'; 'the *any-time* cereal'; 'fifteen *happy-family* menus'.

EMBEDDED ADJECTIVE GROUPS. 'a wholesome, *ready-to-eat* cereal'; 'an *easy-to-paint* picture'; 'that *smart-as-mink* Pink Lady'.

EMBEDDED ADVERBIAL GROUPS. '*all-round* protection'; 'their *up-to-the-minute* styling'; 'that *all-over, under-the-weather* feeling'; 'the *all-round-the-garden* fertiliser'.

EMBEDDED INFINITIVE CLAUSES. 'this eight-page *pull-out* booklet'; 'the *go-anywhere* Electrolux 16 refrigerator'; '*keep-it-up* energy'; 'the new *push-button* weedkiller'.

There seems, in fact, to be very little restriction on the kind of embedded structure than can occur in this pre-modifying position. Compounding is exceptionally free in the noun group not only in lexical productiveness, but also in variety of grammatical structure.

The utility of compound pre-modifiers in advertising is rather difficult to explain; but various suggestions can be made, based upon the foregoing examples and the discussion of pre-modification in the last chapter. Compound pre-modifiers, like noun and adjective pre-modifiers, can be used either attributively or designatively: they can add emotively slanted description, or merely specify more exactly the referential domain of the accompanying noun. Like noun pre-modifiers, their semantic relationship to the head is often not explicitly signalled, as it would be in post-modification: 'feather-light flakes' = 'flakes light as a feather'; 'chocolate-flavoured cereal' = 'cereal flavoured with chocolate'; 'stiff-tufted mud remover' = 'mud remover with stiff tufts'. This compression of meaning can be accompanied, as in the case of noun modifiers, by a certain vagueness. The denotative meaning of 'happy-family (menus)' might be explicated by a long-winded relative clause like '(menus) which help to make a happy family'; whereas 'top-of-the-stove cookery' and 'top-of-the-tree flavour' seem to defy any attempt at paraphrase. With fanciful compounds like these, there is, if anything, a metaphorical connection between the compound and the head. A further speculative reason for the popularity of modifying compounds is that since they function as a single adjective or noun, they are somehow apprehended as designating a single quality. 'Easy-to-read stories' perhaps attributes a special property to 'stories' in a way that 'easy stories to read' or 'stories which are easy to read' does not. This explanation would seem to fit a characteristic use of an embedded noun group compound before a brand-name: '*instant-dispersal* Daxaids'; '*double-action* Clean-Leaf'; 'new *One-action* Swift carpet shampoo'. The compound epithet here seems to denote a special key attribute possessed by the product. Be this as it may, advertising compounds in general represent a departure from commonplace linguistic expression, and seem to add vigour and impact to the advertising message.

Compound Heads

The most productive and widespread type of compound head in English is that which consists of two nouns. *Bedtime, toothbrush,* and *fireplace* are examples of established lexical items on this pattern, but the general proliferation of such compounds in contemporary English, especially in such fields as commerce, government, and technology, extends far beyond the capacity of the largest dictionary. Frequently no hypen is written between the elements, so that in writing the compound is indistinguishable from an N H construction, in which the first noun is a modifier and the second a head. Intonation provides the criterion for separating them: in 'summer term' (N H) the pitch falls on the second noun, whereas in 'summertime' (H compound) it falls on the first. On the same grounds, we would classify 'meat prices', but not 'meat-pie', as a compound, although in this particular instance normal punctuation would give grounds to suppose the reverse. Many noun + noun compounds in advertising have a semi-technical meaning in the description of the product, or the sphere of human activity with which the product is associated. For instance, in a series of three commercials for a brand of refrigerator, the following compounds were used to denote various features of design: 'cheese compartments', 'door shelves', 'ice tray', 'floor stand', 'storage space', 'shelf area', and 'vegetable drawer'. Less practical in purpose are compounds like 'colour freshness', 'jelly addict', and 'man-appeal' (in the slogan 'Oxo gives a meal man-appeal'). In spite of occasional uncustomary formations such as these, one would hesitate to say that this compound pattern is more productive in advertising than in most other varieties of modern English. The urge for neologism seems to manifest itself more in less common types of compound structure: 'quick-knits'; 'speedy-knit'; 'flip-tops'.

Morphology

The general simplicity of word structure in advertising English will emerge from a later study of vocabulary (Chapter 17). At this juncture we will merely note that Romance prefixes and suffixes tend to be of infrequent occurrence, and that the copywriter normally sticks to his maxim of 'preferring the simple word to the complex word'. Only two affixes call for comment. The prefix *super-* is used in a way peculiar to advertising as a means of intensifying an adjective or verb stem: *superfine, superlight, supersified*. The suffix *-y*, which is highly productive in colloquial English, is by far the most frequent adjective suffix in advertising copy. It is used liberally not only in commonplace items like *funny, greedy,* and *happy,* but also in less conventional formations like *bubbly, minty, poppy,* and *oveny*. Something of the variety of these adjectives, and their capacity for sensuous description, can be gathered from the following list of epithets applied to various food products: *chewy, chunky, crackly, creamy, crispy, crumbly, crunchy, flaky, juicy, meaty, milky, minty, nutty, porky, silky, spicy*. Their special value in copywriting seems to derive from a directness of appeal due to their reference to the sensible properties of a product, either of flavour or texture. The suffix has an unusually wide application, being added to noun, adjective, or verb stems (*meaty, crispy, chewy*). It also has denotative ambiguity. Some of the diverse senses one might attach to these words are: 'meaty' = 'full of meat'; 'silky' = 'like silk'; 'chewy' = 'easy to chew'; 'crumbly' = 'inclined to crumble'. In 'lovely, oveny biscuits', 'oveny' can only be made denotatively meaningful by reading in something extra: perhaps '*fresh from* the oven'. But these adjectives, like many of the compounds we have examined, communicate on an evocative, rather than on a cognitive plane.

Chapter 16

Cohesion and Lack of Cohesion

The study of COHESION, in this chapter, will be treated as the study of elements by which the individual logical parts of a message are joined together in coherent discourse.* By 'logical parts', I mean the semantic components which are equivalent in status to propositions in logic, although they may take the form not only of assertions, but of questions, commands, hypotheses, and so on. Thus each of the following sentences expresses an independent statement about John:

> John came yesterday
> John is Mary's brother
> John is Jim's brother

These assertions might be joined in any of the following ways:

> John, who came yesterday, is Mary's and Jim's brother.
> John came yesterday. He's Mary's brother. He's also Jim's brother.
> John – that's Mary's and Jim's brother – came yesterday.

And of course, there are numerous other ways to choose, depending on how a speaker finds it best or easiest to organise his thoughts. Each logical component corresponds roughly to a clause, except where co-ordination is used (as in 'Mary's and Jim's') to compress two or more into a single clause.

Cohesion falls naturally into two divisions: cohesion within the sentence, which includes subordination and co-ordination, and cohesion across sentence boundaries, which is mainly a question of 'pointers' or 'sequence signals' referring back or forward to neighbouring sentences. Grammatical items which often have this function are third person pronouns, demonstratives, and a class of 'conjunctive adjuncts' (*so, also, yet, consequently, by the way, in fact*, etc.). The repetition of a lexical item, or of a whole phrase, may also be considered a variety of cohesion. All these formal means of cross-reference operate not only between sentences, but within single sentences.

---

* Halliday (1964) discusses cohesion in formal rather than semantic terms.

Co-ordination and Subordination of Clauses

In some circumstances, copywriters show unusual tendencies to use

1. co-ordination in preference to subordination, and
2. non-linking co-ordination (parataxis and apposition) in preference to linking co-ordination

where there is an effective choice between these methods of connection.

With regard to the first tendency, we have already noticed that dependent clauses are comparatively infrequent (p. 120), and that co-ordination is sometimes used where subordination would have made the relationship between the clauses more explicit. This is the case with sentences consisting of an imperative linked to an affirmative clause:

> Just water it on, and weeds shoot up, then curl and wither away.

which might be paraphrased by a sentence with a conditional clause: 'If you just water it on, weeds shoot up, then curl and wither away'. There is also a type of sentence in advertising which consists of a pair of imperative clauses in apposition:

> Be prepared! Keep Eno on hand for stomach upsets.

> Lose weight the safe, natural way without being hungry. Ask your chemist for Metercal, and lose up to $\frac{1}{2}$ lb. a day.

> Be sure of yourself. Use Body Mist, the perfumed deodorant.

The assumed relationship between the clauses is that the second action guarantees the first: this, too, might have been expressed by a subordinate clause: 'To be sure of yourself, use Body Mist, the perfumed deodorant'.

The second tendency, that of preferring non-linked to linked co-ordination, concerns the choice between parataxis and linking by the conjunctions *and* and *or*. It is difficult to decide the conditions of parataxis at clause rank (that is, to decide whether two unlinked main clauses are paratactically co-ordinated, or whether they belong to separate sentences). But the problem of recognition does not arise in the case of branching clause parataxis (see p. 18), where two or more clauses share the same subject:

> All Gaymel paints start brighter, stay brighter.

> Bristow's special lanolin replaces the natural oils dry hair lacks. Makes it feel good – look good – silky smooth, and just as you want it.

Its tasteless, non-toxic wax coating prevents sticking – peels off easily after hours in the oven – saves greasing the greaseproof!

That's why they mop spills faster, dry hands more hygenically, wipe working surfaces quicker . . . do most kitchen chores more effectively.

The first two examples are from television commercials, and the second two from the press, where this construction is especially common. As a device for listing the advantages of buying a product, branching clause parataxis is a specialised feature of advertising language. Parataxis is not numerically so frequent as linking, but it is common enough to be regarded as a real alternative in advertising language, whereas in most types of discursive English it is scarcely found at all. It might indeed be regarded as the disjunctive equivalent of linking: it occurs, for example, in tabulated lists, and in displayed headings involving itemisation.

Grammatical Pointers

In a type of language where sentences are short and simple, one would expect the continuity of the message to depend greatly on grammatical pointers, or signals of cross-reference. It was noted on p. 119 that causal connections in advertising are often expressed in the form 'That's why...', instead of by an anticipatory clause of reason. This is the chief function of *that* in advertising copy: to stand on its own as subject of a sentence, and refer back to a preceding part of the text. It can make several other connections besides that of causality: 'That means . . .'; 'That's how . . .'; 'That's what . . .'; 'That's the stuff for hungry folk'; etc. Note that this use of cross-reference does not necessarily help to reduce sentence complexity: dependent 'indirect question' clauses are introduced in sentences like 'That's why so many mothers are using Clinic Shampoo'. However, it does ensure that the message is fed to its audience in small, easily digestible morsels, so that it is very easy to follow and assimilate.

A very characteristic function of *that*, *it*, and *they* in disjunctive television copy is to refer forward or back to a noun group which constitutes a minor clause:

Crisp, tasty Cubs. *They* might have been made for children.

Why not try *it*? Knorr Bean Soup with Tomato.

The pudding with the surprise – *that's* Mary Baker's Sweet-Bake . . .

This shows very clearly how grammatical cross-reference can contribute to the presentation of the message in easy stages. By the replacement of the pronoun or demonstrative by the noun group, each pair of sentences could easily have been reduced to one: 'Crisp tasty Cubs might have been made for your children'. Perhaps the effect is not just to make shorter sentences, but to give isolative emphasis to each 'morsel' of the message, and especially to the noun group, which usually refers to the product being advertised.

The conjunctive adverb *so* and the conjunction *because*, which in some respects behaves as a conjunctive adverb, were discussed in Chapter 12 (see pp. 118-19). Other conjunctive adjuncts are rare, especially the phrasal ones much used in formal composition: 'in addition', 'as a result', etc.

Grammatical cross-reference, except for the cases mentioned, has a comparatively unimportant role in advertising English, which follows the pattern of colloquial English in frequently letting the relationship between sentences be assumed, instead of overtly expressed. Even signals of the reason-consequence relation are not very frequent, considering how fundamental this relation is to the semantics of advertising:

> Hennessy brandy is distilled in Cognac, blended in Cognac and bottled in Cognac. No brandy could be more French.

Here, and in countless other cases, the implicit 'That's why'is unexpressed. The presence of visual material also reduces the role of grammatical cohesion. The deictic items *this, that, these, those, here, there* can be used to refer either to the linguistic context (cross-reference) or to the non-linguistic context – to illustrations in the press, or to the visual sequence in commercials. In the television sample, all these items except *that* were mainly used in the latter function. This is one indication that there is less demand for continuity in the text when visual material provides a focus for reference.

Lexical cohesion, in the form of repetitions of proper names and lexical items, is a different matter. Persistent iteration of brand-names and other items in advertising has a more obvious function than that of providing continuity. However, it does incidentally serve this purpose, and repetitions of a brand-name often occur in neighbouring clauses, where in normal circumstances the repetition would be avoided by the use of a pronoun:

> But be sure to use *Span*, because *Span Medicated Shampoo* is specially made for town living.

And *Clark's sandals* really fit, because *Clark's sandals* are made in four width fittings.

The repetition is particularly associated with *because* clauses, as illustrated in these examples.

Co-ordination of Groups

Co-ordination at group rank is an especially important cohesional factor in advertising language, where, at least in more disjunctive kinds of copy, the group tends to be the largest unit to play a significant role in communication.

The three types of co-ordination, linking, parataxis, and apposition, all have prominent roles in advertising. Linking, whether by the conjunctions *and* or *or*, has the obvious function of enumerating the various properties, ingredients, uses, etc. of the product:

> For *sugar beet, spring wheat and spring barley*, you need C.C.F. *Nitrogen Phosphate and Potash* for *vigorous growth, strong roots and healthy crops*.

Parataxis, although semantically equivalent to linking, is perhaps a little vaguer: sometimes it is not clear whether the appropriate conjunction to insert would be *and* or *or*. Parataxis of groups is found in spontaneous informal speech: it is 'open-ended', in the sense that the speaker may continue to add to his list even after he has reached the point where he intended to finish it.* Linking, on the other hand, suggests a degree of premeditation: the conjunction, preceding the last element of the list, is an anticipatory clue that the series is about to come to an end. In advertising, there is of course no question of spontaneity, but perhaps the implication of a list to which more items could be added if desired has a rhetorical effect in sentences such as:

> Here's all the information – *weight, riders, recent performance* – all so easy to follow.
>
> *Wonderful cold dishes, iced drinks, children's favourite treats.* A new world of luxury opens with an Electrolux refrigerator.

A more obvious rhetorical note is sounded in cases where the co-ordinate groups show close formal parallelism:

---

* See Jespersen (1924), p. 27.

Your baby needs the softness of Lux-washed woollies, the safety of Lux-washed nappies.

Soft colours. Glowing colours. Shy colours. Bold colours. Beautifully new, up-to-the-modern-minute colours.

In press advertising, noun group parataxis has a more mundane function in conjunction with display, for example in the listing of the addresses of the advertising firm: 'New York – Paris – London'. Parataxis of adjective groups is also common, and serves the same kind of purpose as the listing of pre-modifying adjectives in a noun group: 'Bubbly Stergene, soft – gentle – safe – essential for all your finest things'.

We turn now to the third type of co-ordination, apposition. A construction highly characteristic of advertising copy is the apposition of two noun groups, one of which names the product: 'Lifeguard. The disinfectant you trust completely'; 'Churchman's Olympic Tipped – the cigarette that leads the way'; 'the new Ronson C.F.L. – the shaver with the golden touch'. In the television sample, one in every two or three commercials contained an example of this construction, which also sometimes occurs as a signature line in press advertisements. Its function is obviously to associate the brand-name with a 'tag-line' expressing an appealing and distinctive image of the product. In the above cases, the product name precedes the noun group which describes it. The reverse order also occurs, but with less frequency: 'an altogether new kind of sweet. Pascall Butter Fruits'.

A special kind of apposition common in television advertising is a structure in which a group is partially or exactly repeated. As would be expected, it most often takes the form of a repetition of the brand-name:

Get it off with *Dabitoff*. *Dabitoff*. *Dabitoff*.

When the wind has a bite – and you feel like a bite – then bite on *a Whole Nut – Cadbury's Whole Nut* – the chocolate that gives you something to bite on.

Iterative apposition in jingles is taken to extremes which would be absurd in speech or writing:

> Lucky Charm, Lucky Charm
> For every date and every day
> Well – the nylons to wear are Lucky Charm
> Lucky, Lucky, Lucky Charm.

> Never, never, never,
> Never go, go, go,
> Never go without, never go without
> A Capstan Capstan Capstan . . .

The repeated segments may be words, groups, clauses, sentences, or (as in the case of 'never go without') may not coincide with any grammatical unit.

Noun apposition is sometimes discontinuous: that is to say, one of the elements is postponed to the end of the clause, and separated from its fellow by other structural constituents. Here the two noun groups are separated by an adverbial group:

> Have *some Harveys* with your Christmas – *the most distinguished sherries you can buy.*

This is again a respect in which advertising language resembles impromptu speech, where the discontinuity seems to arise from the desire to add an afterthought to an already complete remark: 'I've asked the Browns to come – the people we met at the play'. But in advertising, it is best explained as a means of avoiding parenthetical structure, and perhaps of placing the final element in a conspicuous position at the end of the sentence, where emphasis will naturally fall.

Cohesion in the Disjunctive Mode

Through co-ordination, sentences in advertising copy which are otherwise simple sometimes attain considerable length. Indeed, this aspect of grammatical structure rather spoils the picture of the simplicity of advertising language which has so far been painted. Co-ordinative complexity, however, is a very different order of complexity from that of place ordered structure, dependence, or embedding, and it might be better to refer to it by a separate term – perhaps 'prolixity'. This would avoid the implication that co-ordinative depth has something to do with involved subject-matter and difficulties of comprehension. The kind of listing made in this commercial, for instance, communicates at a very elementary level, and calls for the minimum degree of active concentration from the audience:

> News pictures – action pictures – funny pictures – human pictures – happy pictures – all the great pictures of 1960 – in a 4 page extra, in tomorrow's Sunday Dispatch.

Even longer sentences than this are built up in disjunctive advertising copy by combinations of different types of co-ordination.

However, it is difficult to assign co-ordinative relationships at higher ranks in disjunctive grammar, where the only recognition cues for apposition and parataxis are provided only by orthography, phonology, or semantics. It is also difficult to decide at what rank co-ordinative structures operate. In a sentence such as 'Olivier – the tipped cigarette for go-ahead people', should the apposition be described as an apposition of minor clauses or of groups? That is, does the sentence consist of two minor clauses each consisting of one group, or of one minor clause consisting of two groups? This dilemma arises only because the five grammatical ranks required for the description of the English language as a whole are not fully implemented in disjunctive language. But as the test of 'disjunctivity' is the extent to which a text can be described without reference to higher ranks (see pp. 91–3), a co-ordinative relationship should be assigned to the lowest rank possible: in the case above, to group instead of clause rank.

Because of the indeterminacy of the boundaries of clauses and sentences in disjunctive advertising grammar, cohesion in disjunctive copy can best be studied by concentrating on the relation between the largest units which have definitive structures: mostly groups and non-finite clauses. 'Cohesion', however, must be understood in a slightly altered sense. The group, the most important unit in disjunctive copy, is 'sub-logical' in the sense that it does not on its own have the semantic structure of a proposition. On the other hand, there are implied logical relations between groups in sequence, and these can be explicit in a 'translation' into discursive English. Apposition implies referential equivalence, so 'Olivier – the tipped cigarette for go-ahead people' might be discursively rendered 'Olivier is the tipped cigarette for go-ahead people'. An adjective and a noun group together can similarly be collapsed into a single clause by the use of the verb to be: 'Nimble bread – delicious – light as a feather' becomes (making use of the semantic equivalence of parataxis and linking) 'Nimble bread is delicious and light as a feather'. By a similar change combined with rearrangement, 'Made from the whole wheat grain, Whole Wheat Flakes' becomes 'Whole Wheat Flakes are made from the whole wheat grain'. These imputed semantic relations can be exemplified collectively in a more extended piece of copy (in fact, the whole script for a thirty-second commercial):

Kellogg's Frosties. So crisp and refreshing, Sparkling with a snowy

> sugar frosting. Toasted to a golden crispness. Kellogg's Frosties. The
> crisp breakfast.

which might be rendered into discursive English in three sentences:

> Kellogg's Frosties are so crisp and refreshing. They sparkle with a
> snowy sugar frosting, and are toasted to a golden crispness. Kellogg's
> Frosties are the crisp breakfast.

This, of course, is only one of many possible 'translations' which would
preserve the implicit meaning of the original.

But it is necessary to inquire into the nature of these 'translations'. Are
they based on complete semantic equivalence? The denotative meaning is
the same, but the discursive version has an added logical content. This can
be illustrated by comparing three similar pieces of language:

> delicious, light-as-a-feather Nimble bread.
>
> Nimble bread. Delicious, light as a feather.
>
> Nimble bread is delicious and light as a feather.

All have the same denotative content; the first clearly is not a statement,
whereas the third is. The second version belongs with the first, rather than
the third: it has no interrogative equivalent, as the third has ('Is Nimble
bread delicious and light as a feather?'), by which its truth or falsehood
can be questioned.

From the earlier discussion of assumed causal and conditional connections, it is evident that any semantic analysis of a natural language such as
English would have to allow for 'imputed' semantic relations which are
not overtly signalled, and arise simply from juxtaposition. In disjunctive
language, these relations are of a more atomistic character: they do not
operate on propositions, but are themselves the components of which
propositions are made. But there is a difference between what is actually
expressed, and what has to be interpretatively supplied. Disjunctive copy
communicates at a 'sub-logical' level and helps in the reinforcement of the
associative, as opposed to the cognitive side of the message.

Chapter 17

Vocabulary: Verbs and Adjectives

In this chapter I report some of the significant findings of a vocabulary analysis of my sample of television advertisements. The main part of the analysis was a simple operation: it consisted in counting occurrences of the same item, where 'the same item' means the same lexical item functioning in the same word class. Thus *fight* as a noun and *fight* as a verb would be considered different items. This also meant excluding items extending over more than one word: *make sure, put off, take care*, etc. However, this was not such a limitation as it might appear, for though many such idioms are found in advertising copy, none of them is frequent enough to effect the results presented here.

The study of vocabulary in these terms is confined to classes of word which are productive and have an indefinitely large membership: nouns, verbs (excluding *be*), adjectives, and certain types of adverb. This discussion, however, will be restricted still further to the two classes which reveal most specialisation of vocabulary: adjectives and verbs. These classes have an additional contrastive interest, in that advertising language is marked by a wealth of adjective vocabulary, and a poverty of verb vocabulary.

We have to beware, here as elsewhere, of adopting too rigid a notion of specialisation. It is tempting to think that copywriters adhere to a 'stock vocabulary' of items which are used over and over again. 'Favourite vocabulary' would be a better terminological choice, for whereas copywriters show strong lexical preferences, they certainly have no aversion to using unusual items, and, as we saw in the study of compounds, a search for striking and vivid forms of expression may take them beyond the established range of lexical items in the English language.

Adjective Vocabulary

The twenty most common adjectives in direct address advertising, in order of frequency, were:

1. *new*	11. *crisp*
2. *good/better/best*	12. *fine*
3. *free*	13. *big*
4. *fresh*	14. *great*
5. *delicious*	15. *real*
6. { *full* / *sure* }	16. { *easy* / *bright* }
8. { *clean* / *wonderful* }	18. { *extra* / *safe* }
10. *special*	20. *rich*

The first item on the list, *new*, is a word which apparently cannot be used too often. Its ubiquitous application is seen in the fact that it collocated with common nouns referring to a wide range of products and product accessories: *booklet, bottle, car, fishsteaks, newspaper, shampoo, soup, toothbrush, tyre, weedkiller,* and many more. It is also significant that in more than a third of its occurrences, *new* combined with the name of the advertised product. Amongst the abstract nouns with which it occurred are *contest, competition, ideas,* and a number of nouns referring to attributes of the product: *sizes, shape, look, tingle, brilliance, colour, formula,* etc. It seems to be attributable to any aspect of the product.

Good/better/best might appear to be another all-purpose epithet, particularly in its comparative and superlative forms. It is something of a surprise, then, to find that it collocates with only two kinds of product: food and tobacco. With food, it has the connotation of 'wholesomeness', whereas with other products a more specific and colourful laudatory adjective is preferred. *Good* also collocates with a number of nouns which do not denote a product, but have reference to food: *food* itself, *breakfast, flavour, gravy, sandwich,* etc. The use of *good* with cigarettes and tobacco probably reflects the difficulty of finding more specific grounds on which to commend this class of product.

Good and *new* are over twice as popular as any other adjective. Of the remaining members of the list, *wonderful, fine,* and (in many instances) *great,* are adjectives of general commendation, whereas others are associated with particular product groups, and demonstrate the tendency to choose a commendatory adjective especially appropriate to the type of product. *Delicious, crisp, fresh,* and *rich* are key words in food advertising, and their frequency reflects the high proportion of television advertising devoted to foodstuffs. (Also, the television sample was slightly skewed, in containing a higher percentage than usual of commercials for food and drink.) *Fresh* and *clean* are favourite items in toothpaste advertisements, and the latter adjective applies also to many kinds of cleaning products: detergents, soaps, shampoos, and so on. *Sure* is the only one of the twenty items used more in reference to persons than things. *Safe* and *sure* are inevitable items to use in connection with products to do with hygiene, such as germicides, deodorants, and detergents. They can be employed with iterative emphasis:

> This baby's nappy is Lux-safe. Safe with the safety that you get with pure soap.

> You're sure of personal freshness – lasting day and night freshness – and sure of a lovely, lingering perfume. This winter – be sure. Use double-sure Body Mist, the perfumed deodorant.

Extra and *special* have a function similar to that of *new*: they express the 'differentness' of the claim made on behalf of the product. *Free*, naturally enough, never occurs with a brand-name or noun denoting an advertised product. Its main use is in connection with an added material inducement to the purchaser: a 'free offer' of one kind or another.

Delicious, good and *fresh*, as adjectives used to recommend food products, sometimes underline the pleasurable associations of more specific adjectives in their environment. *Delicious*, for instance, occurs with adjectives like *chunky, crisp, crunchy, flaky, homemade, juicy*, and *light*. In 'good honest plain flour' and 'good quick sandwich', the commendatory adjective seems to transfer its connotative value so as to bring out the favourable, rather than unfavourable associations of *plain* and *quick*.

Now a word on adjectives which are conspicuous by their absence from this list, and from the standard vocabulary of advertising in general. It is scarcely necessary to observe that the utility of commendatory adjectives in advertising is matched by the inappropriateness of pejorative ones. The high frequency of *good/better/best* contrasts with a very low frequency of its antonym *bad/worse/worst*. In fact against nearly a hundred occurrences of *good* there was not a single occurrence of *bad* in direct address in the television sample. If *bad* is avoided, the pejorative counterparts of adjectives of more enthusiastic praise (*ghastly, dreadful*, etc. as opposed to *wonderful, delicious*, etc.) are even less likely.

That certain commendatory adjectives are preferred to others is less easy to explain. *Good* and *wonderful* are many times more common than *nice* and *marvellous*. The latter two, however, are popular in indirect address advertising, apparently being better suited to the language of secondary participants. *Lovely* is another epithet used more in indirect than in direct address; its application in direct address advertising is mainly in the more specific sense of 'beautiful'.

Verb Vocabulary

The twenty most common verbs in the television sample were all very commonplace English monosyllables, and all except one (*use*) belonged to the Germanic stock which has remained up to the present day the core of colloquial English verb vocabulary:

1. *make*	8. *go*	15. $\begin{cases} feel \\ like \end{cases}$
2. *get*	9. *know*	
3. *give*	10. $\begin{cases} keep \\ look \end{cases}$	17. *choose*
4. *have*		18. *take*
5. *see*	12. *need*	19. $\begin{cases} start \\ taste \end{cases}$
6. *buy*	13. *love*	
7. *come*	14. *use*	

Although at first glance there is nothing remarkable about this list, certain verbs in particular (*get, make, give, like, love, buy, need, use*) owe their position in it partly to their special application to the advertising situation. An invented piece of copy which incorporates all these verbs shows roughly what their special functions are:

> Buy X. Use it. It's made by Y. X will give you what you need. You'll like X. In fact you'll love it. Get X.

I do not intend to defend this essay in copywriting against the charge of egregious ineptitude. In fact, part of its illustrative value is that it shows how little an advertisement says when the meanings conveyed by adjectives and nouns are pruned away. Many of the verbs in this list have a very general meaning, and contribute little to the force of an advertising message. They are the 'bare pegs' on which descriptions of the product and its effects are loaded.

Simplicity of verbal meaning can be associated with the morphological simplicity of verbs (very few verbs in advertising have affixes), and the structural simplicity of the verbal group. In fact, in whatever linguistic application 'verb' is used, its function in advertising language is inconspicuous. Advertising has furthermore developed its own disjunctive variety of English, in which verbs do not need to be used at all.

In an analysis of the use of these common English verbs, it must be borne in mind that many of them have varying grammatical functions, and meanings that vary accordingly. Nevertheless, some general observations can be made about them. Over half of them fit into the by now familiar pattern of advertising discourse, in that one of their functions is to denote a relationship between consumer and product. *Have, get, give, buy,* and *keep* have to do with the possession of the product: *have* and *have got* convey an idea of neutral possession; *keep* continuing possession; *buy* and *get* acquisition; *give* the conferring of possession on somebody else (this item becomes extra prominent during the Christmas shopping season). Another group of verbs has to do with consumption: *take, use,* and (in one of its uses) *have. Like, love,* and *need* denote mental disposition towards the product, and *choose* and *taste* indicate other links between product and consumer. Members of all these groups are commonly used in the imperative, or with *you* as a subject. But verbs connected with possession also often have a prominent use when the subject refers to the product itself: 'It's got a sparkle in the middle'; 'Oxo gives a meal manappeal' etc. In this case, the verb has an attributive function, indicating how the product possesses or confers properties which are distinctive or valuable to the consumer. Similarly, *look, feel,* and *taste* can be descriptive of the consumer's sensations or feelings ('Taste the tang in Tango') or, with an inanimate subject, can describe the sensible properties of the product: 'Cyril Lord Standard Carpet feels so soft'.

Chapter 18

Some Questions of Semantics

Part of the skill of copywriting lies in what might be called 'strategic semantics': the art of conveying meanings which contribute to the selling effectiveness of an advertisement, and avoiding those which detract from it. Some elementary strategies of this kind have been mentioned, and will receive no further comment: they include the expression of certainty rather than doubt; of positive rather than negative ideas; of commendatory rather than pejorative attributes. Now we shall see how some other semantic categories are put to special use in the advertising situation.

Particularity of Reference

Particularity, or uniqueness, of reference is a semantic property of proper names, and also of a number of grammatical items such as personal pronouns, demonstratives, the definite article, and the adverbs *here, there, now*, and *then*. These grammatical items 'name' in the sense that they refer to, or rather point to, some entity, entities, place, time, etc., given or understood from their context. Theirs is a 'showing', or DEICTIC function. The context to which they refer may be either linguistic or non-linguistic. We saw on pp. 144–5 how both these types of contextual reference helped to explain the function of demonstratives in advertising.

Both proper and deictic names have a crucial role in most kinds of discourse, and this is especially so in advertising language. A type of proper name, a brand-name, is used to refer to the product; and a type of deictic name, the second person pronoun, is used to refer to the consumer. Without these two naming operations, advertising copy would scarcely be recognisable as advertising copy. But do the pronoun *you* and the brand-name meet the requirement of particularity of reference? *You* refers to a host of readers and viewers; a brand-name refers to a vast number of specimens of the same article. To this objection we can reply that both are generally treated as if they were unique: *the* product, not a class of articles bearing the same label; and *the* person being addressed, not just anyone.

Deictic items are used not only when the uniqueness of the referent is contextually determined, but when it is a matter of subjective assumption, or is consequent to the nature of the reference. To me, '*the* postman' means the man who brings letters to my door; to you he may be quite a different individual. In 'the first astronaut' and 'the richest man in the world', uniqueness is inherent in the meaning of *first* and the superlative adjective *richest*; 'a richest man in the world' would be a contradiction. The definite article is characteristically employed in advertising in this sense of *absolute* deixis, without reference either to the linguistic or non-linguistic context. Most appositional constructions which have the brand-name as their first element contain this kind of *the* in the other element: 'Wisdom. The "correct shaped" toothbrush'; 'Condor Sliced – the flake with the flavour'; 'Twink – the home perm with the built-in oil-con-ditioner'. These constructions have the character of particular definitions; they equate one kind of name, a brand-name, with another – an expression describing some unique entity. Their implicit force was clarified by Bertrand Russell when he rendered 'Scott was the author of *Waverley*' into a kind of logical discourse as 'One and only one entity wrote *Waverley*, and Scott was identical with that one'.* Although the equative relation is implied, rather than overtly asserted, in the appositional struc-ture, 'Wisdom. The "correct shaped" toothbrush' in effect conceals a supposition that all other toothbrushes are wrongly shaped.

The definite article's implication of uniqueness can also be used to advantage in references to the consumer. One advertisement carries the headline 'Be the girl with the Bush transistor portable'. Here there is no particularity in the obvious sense: the advertiser is not offering anyone the opportunity to become the sole owner of his product. However, two other interpretations suggest themselves. In the first place, *the* is often used in a generic sense, as I have used it in 'the copywriter', 'the product', 'the consumer' throughout this book. Generic *the* attributes uniqueness to a whole class of entities, not to any particular member of it. If 'the girl' is understood in this way, the headline is an invitation to become a member of a particular class of girl. The body copy which follows upholds this interpretation, by listing the enviable qualities by which the class is dis-tinguished:

Be the girl with the Bush. Beautiful. Clever. The perfect partner.

Secondly, *the* might, with a certain degree of semantic licence, have the

* Bertrand Russell, 'On denoting', *Mind*, 14 (1905); reprinted in *Readings in Philo-sophical Analysis*, ed. H. Feigl and W. Sellars, (New York, 1949), p. 111.

interpretation of subjectively assumed uniqueness, as in the case of 'the postman'. We imagine the girl having distinction in attractiveness and prestige with her own circle as 'the girl with the Bush'. This interpretation appears to fit in with the illustration, which shows a girl sitting on the ground with her portable radio, while three young men eye her from behind a tree.

That is another deictic item which is used with the force of absolute uniqueness:

> A Green Shield Worthington gives every man *that* great feeling.

> That's why outside your house or inside your home – Gaymel paint with its brilliant gloss, starts brighter, and keeps *that* bright fresh look year after year after year.

Used in this way, *that* usually modifies an abstract noun of sensation, and 'that X' conveys something like 'the X which cannot fail to strike every user of the product as different from other Xs'.

There is some kinship between these special senses of *the* and *that*, and the use of *such* and *so* in sentences like 'Such a good natural cheddar'; 'Fresh dairy cream tastes so good'; 'It keeps your toilet so bright'. The sub-modifier *so* is very often used in this way, as an emotive intensifier to an adjective, rather than as a marker introducing a clause of extent ('so good that . . .'). In the latter case, the deictic force of *so* is captured in a paraphrase containing *the*: 'good to the extent that . . .'. When *so* is not followed by the *that* clause, it might be claimed that the deictive function is still present in an absolute sense, and that the full denotative value of 'so good' could be expressed as 'good to a unique extent'. However, in ordinary conversation, as in advertising, this force of *so* is somewhat weakened by its hyperbolic use to express an emotional attitude.

Before leaving the subject of particularity of reference, we might notice the frequency in advertising of items which express uniqueness in a more direct way: the adjective *unique* itself ('the unique prescription for colds and 'flu'); superlative adjectives; and *only* ('the only chocolate flavoured cereal'). These reveal their connection with deixis in always following *the* in the noun group, except in special usages like 'a best man' or 'an only child'. Then there are the already mentioned phrases 'no other' and 'nothing else', whose value in expressing exclusiveness outweighs their disadvantage in being negative. All these are means of emphasising the unique advantage of a product over its competitors.

Universality of Reference

Now we move from one extreme to another; from the most exclusive to the most inclusive mode of reference. Universality of reference is often assumed where no definite limit to the applicability of a meaning is implied: 'Men are sinners' is taken as a statement about the whole human race, if only because there is no qualification, as in 'some men' or 'men who gamble', to indicate the contrary. To this extent, the present tense in advertising typically implies unlimited time reference (see pp. 123–4). But there are also items which positively assert universality: *all*, *every*, and words containing these forms, like *always*, *everyone*, *everything*; and *no* (as a determiner), *none*, *never*, *nobody*, etc. are categorically exclusive in meaning, combining universality with negation.

Items of positive universal meaning are especially common in advertising copy. *All* and *every*, for example, are by far the most common determiners excluding articles and demonstratives. 'Its instant germ-killing action kills *all* germs twelve times faster'; 'There's a fertiliser for *every* crop you grow and for *every* soil, in Fison's 40 Range'. The related items *always* and *everyone* are illustrated in 'She *always* uses Kraft superfine margarine' and '*Everyone* loves Hartley's Jam'.

The universal negators *no*, *never*, etc. are less than half as frequent as *all*, *every*, and their related forms, but are certainly not under the same interdiction as the simple negative *not*. An advertising message may be negatively orientated, in the sense that it bases its appeal to the consumer not on what she wants, but on what she wants to get rid of. In this case, *no* and *never* can emphasise how the product offers a *complete* cure for some particular ill. In the following commercial, the opening shot shows a saucepan of milk boiling over:

> Never again. Look! No more boiling over. Here's the burner that thinks for itself. Look! The Magitrol, only on the Renown 7. The Parkinson Cowan Renown 7. Look in your gas showroom now.

Never combined with a further negative implication can have the effect of uncompromising positiveness; 'Never go to bed with a cold without decongestant Vick Vapour Rub' is notionally equivalent to 'Always go to bed . . . with Vick Vapour Rub'. However, not all items in this group are useful in advertising: there were no occurrences of the animate forms *no one* and *nobody* in my sample of direct address television copy.

Items of universal reference evidently serve the copywriter's need to make his claims about the product as comprehensive as possible. One wonders if a challenge to his veracity would often bring a less dogmatic reply, as was the case with Gilbert's Captain Corcoran: 'What never?' 'Well, hardly ever'. But this would be to place too precise a value on these items, which are often used in colloquial speech, and in advertising, with the vague intensifying force of an expansive gesture: 'Here's *all* the flavour of fine Virginia tobacco'; '*Everything* goes with H.P. Sauce'.

Vagueness of Reference

It would be a pity to omit from this study some appraisal of the charge of vagueness often made against advertising language, even though 'vagueness' might itself be open to this charge as a semantic concept. Rather than attempt a definition of 'vagueness', I shall list some facets of advertising language which have already in some context or other come under discussion, and to which the term might reasonably be applied.

1. Disjunctive language, I suggested on p. 150, is a way of communicating on a 'sub-logical' plane, to which judgements of truth and falsehood are not applicable. In using this kind of language, a copywriter does not have to face a potential challenger who asks 'Is this so, or is it not so?' – and the capability of meeting this challenge is one plausible interpretation of semantic precision.

2. Word and compound formation, as discussed in Chapter 15, involves setting up semantic relations which are obscure and open to multiple ambiguity. This is one respect in which advertising copy approaches the poetic function of language, throwing the burden of communication on the imaginative power of words, rather than their denotative content.

3. Evaluative meaning, chiefly expressed in advertising by such adjectives as *good*, *wonderful*, and *delicious*, is vague in the sense that its value ultimately rests on subjective opinion.

4. Unqualified comparatives, such as 'You'll have *fresher* breath, *healthier* teeth and *whiter* teeth' are a well-known feature of advertising copy. Randolph Quirk in *The Use of English* (p. 223) comments on an advertiser's claim 'Scientific experiments have proved that our product makes your clothes whiter' as follows: 'But what . . . are the experiments said to have proved? That "our product" makes clothes "whiter". Makes them whiter than *what*, we must ask. Whiter than when washed under precisely similar conditions using every other relevant product on the

market? Or merely whiter than when they are washed in cold water without soap? Or perhaps, indeed, just whiter than they were before they were washed!' This brings home the point that comparative adjectives are vague – almost, one might say, to the point of meaninglessness – without a standard of comparison. The use of unrelated comparisons, if not the use of attributive adjectives in general, is one of the vaguenesses with which we operate quite happily in ordinary conversation. It is only when faced with language which has designs upon us that we need to regard them with suspicion.

In fact, we need to recognize that all kinds of discourse in natural language (as opposed to logical, mathematical, or other forms of symbolic notation) are vague by any standard of exactitude imposed by philosophical semantics, and that this is not necessarily an evil. Vagueness is such an inevitable concomitant of ordinary linguistic communication, that the result of waging constant war against it, as in science and the law, is a type of language that is unintelligible to all but the expert. Advertising language is not especially imprecise, nor does it contain sources of vagueness not harmlessly present in most other roles of discourse. What sometimes makes vagueness insidious in advertising language, as in other types of loaded language, is the power to mislead, by giving empty claims an appearance of exactitude.

Part Three Change and Creativity

Chapter 19

A Glance at History

A digression on the historical background to modern advertising language can be excused on the grounds both of its intrinsic interest and of its relevance to a 'standard' in advertising language. The conventions which make up 'standard advertising English' can be explained either by their present-day selling effectiveness, or by the force of tradition. Not that these two exclude one another; it can be supposed that at least some techniques of salesmanship belong to all places and times, and apply just as much to modern conditions as to any others. But there is also a certain force of conservatism in advertising practice, which can be attributed to a reluctance to abandon time-tested methods until newer techniques have thoroughly proved themselves. We would therefore like to know where these advertising conventions came from. Are they so inseparable from advertising as to be associated with it from the earliest times, or can we point to a time of, and reason for, their origin?

Change

Large-scale consumer advertising as we know it today developed in the latter half of the nineteenth century.* Prominent among the factors which led to its growth in Britain were the abolition of the tax on newspapers and advertising in 1855, and the extension of basic education to all sections of the society. The 'ordinary housewife', the primary target of consumer advertising today was scarcely within reach of an advertiser until both these changes had taken effect.

The period of the rise of modern advertising was naturally a period of innovation and experiment in linguistic techniques; in fact it was the period which saw the beginning of copywriting as an acknowledged profession. By the 1920s, however, the character of modern advertising

---

* The history of advertising is documented, from varying points of view, in Sampson (1874), Presbrey (1929), Elliott (1962), and Turner (1965). This chapter is based largely on examples and historical background given in the books by Sampson and Presbrey.

copy had emerged, and no important changes in language, apart from the development of iterative techniques associated with broadcast advertising, seem to have taken place since then.

One of the big changes in advertising copy during the transitional period was the evolution of a public-colloquial style, partly through American influence. But the change was slow in taking effect. As late as 1914, some advertisers in 'better magazines' were still adhering to the latinate diction which characterised written English in the eighteenth and nineteenth centuries, as can be seen in this extract from a bicycle advertisement in the *London Illustrated News* in that year:

> Much, however, depends on the machine, therefore select the proved best – the Triumph.

The formality is the only thing that distinguishes this from standard copy of today. Rendering it into colloquial English simply by a substitution of relevant words and phrases will yield a sentence which might easily be found in an advertisement of the 1960s:

> But a lot depends on the machine, so choose the proved best – the Triumph.

Other stock advertising phrases of that period are quaintly formal by modern standards: 'unexcelled quality', 'in a supreme degree', 'is similar in every respect to', 'and kindred ailments' (following a list of diseases in medicine advertisements).

In comparing modern press copy with that used prior to 1850, we need to remember that most advertising of those days was conducted on the lines of the 'classifieds' of today, that its readership was comparatively small and select, and that its initiators were mainly small merchants and private individuals. In this advertisement from the first issue of *The Times* (under that title) on 1 January 1788, we notice greater differences of style; not only in formality, but in impersonality and ceremoniousness:

> VICKERY respectfully informs the ladies that he has now for sale an extensive and admirable assortment of Transparent Tetes, as may be seen by visiting either his Western or Eastern Magazines. The taste, fancy, elegance, convenience, and accommodations of these articles have already rendered them the greatest favourites of every court of Europe, and of numbers in Asia, Africa, and America. Nothing can prove their utility more than their being so secured to the head that the rudest wind will not in the least derange them. Ladies who order

these beautiful articles are requested to describe whether for young, middle-aged, or elderly ladies. *No. 6, Tavistock Street,* and *No. 19, Bishopsgate Street,* near the London Tavern.

N.B. – He has also the greatest assortment of braids ready made at all prices.

Notable contrasts with modern copy are observed in the tokens of tradesmanly deference 'respectfully' and 'are requested to'; the third person address to 'the ladies'; and the enumeration of the product's qualities by abstract nouns rather than by adjectives ('taste, fancy, elegance, convenience, and accommodations'). The construction of 'their being so secured . . .' (gerundive clause with a subject in the genitive case) is too formal in modern English to appear in consumer advertising. The same applies to the verb *rendered* (instead of *made*) and the adjectives *extensive* and *admirable*, which have given way to more colloquial words of similar effect, such as *wonderful, great,* and *fine.* The clause beginning 'Ladies who order these beautiful articles are requested . . .' is a circuitously impersonal equivalent of the blunt modern imperative.

Going further back into advertising history, we come across styles of copy which are even more curious by the standards of modern advertising. One of the first Englishmen to make commercial advertising a business was John Houghton, who in 1692 started a bulletin entitled *The Collection for Improvement of Husbandry and Trade.** As a pioneer, Houghton made up his own advertising conventions as he went along. They included the preservation of the advertiser's anonymity, and reference to himself in the first person:

> I know a peruke maker that pretends to make perukes extraordinary fashionable and will sell good pennyworths; I can direct to him.

This secretive method of advertising, although Houghton made a living out of it for some time, appears in retrospect to have violated the first and unalterable principle of copywriting practice: announcing the name and origin of the advertised product. What made it feasible was an arrangement whereby Houghton himself provided details to applicants, acting as a go-between as modern journals with box-numbers do for personal advertising today. Another oddity of his approach was that of regarding himself an independent arbiter of the quality of the goods advertised. A note of reservation is sounded above in the word *pretends* (in its obsolete

---

* Sampson (1874), pp. 83–92; Presbrey (1929), pp. 56–61.

sense 'claims'). Persuasion had no part in his announcements, and indeed the advertising situation he set up differed in one vital respect from the situation in which advertising as we know it operates: the 'agent' who composed the advertisement was not just a spokesman for the advertiser, but an independent participant, neutral between advertiser and consumer.

Continuity

This excursion through the more recent to the more distant past of advertising may have given the impression that no linguistic 'universals' are to be found in advertising in all phases of its history. But at least one common feature of modern copy has a history stretching back to the remotest origins of written advertising. It is the introductory *if* clause which serves to call out those members of the public to whom an appeal is relevant. This very feature gave a name to the earliest recorded type of written advertisement in English. In the fifteenth and sixteenth centuries, the *'siquis'* (Latin 'if anybody') was a hand-written public notice advertising personal offers and needs, as well as articles for sale.* 'Si quis' had been a conventional opening for lost and found notices in ancient Rome, and its English translation became equally standard for the notices to which it referred in Tudor England. 'If anyone' was incidentally a favourite opening for Houghton and for small advertisers of even later times. The first printed advertisement in English, in which Caxton publicised his edition of the *Saliburi Pye*, began with a variant of this formula:

> If it plese ony man spirituel or temporel to bye ony pyes of two and thre comemoraciõs of salisburi use enpryntid after the forme of this presēt lettre whiche ben wel and truly correct, late hym come to westmonester in to the almonesrye at the reed pale and he shal have them good chepe.
>
> Supplico stet cedula

To bring the *siquis* formula up to date, all that is needed is a substitution of the second person forms *you* and *your* for the indefinite forms *anyone* or *any*.

Another apparently timeless ingredient of advertising language is a pronounced frequency of evaluative and other attributive adjectives, especially in the superlative form. The credit for developing the selling

---

* Sampson (1874), pp. 52–4; Presbrey (1929), pp. 14–18.

potential of superlatives and exaggerated language generally has been accorded to Phineas Barnum, the nineteenth-century American showman and impresario whose circus, 'The Greatest Show on Earth', epitomised in its title the feature we are discussing. But superlatives, whether un-modified or accompanied by an intensifying modification, seem to have always had a prominent place in the language of salesmanship. In a fifteenth-century ballad *London Lickpenny* by Thomas Lydgate, the hero is urged by Cheapside mercers to buy 'Paris thread, the finest in the land'.*
The already quoted *Times* advertisement of 1788 contains three super-latives, and in 'the greatest favourite of every court in Europe, and of numbers in Asia, Africa and America', its author fell short of Barnum's global claim only in omitting Australasia, whose coasts Captain Cook had explored only a few years before.

American Influences

Other characteristics of modern advertising language are also associated with particular American practitioners. The introduction of repetition as a conscious device in copywriting came about adventitiously, through a reluctance of newspapers, both in the U.S.A. and in Britain, to accept display advertising. By tradition, all advertisements were printed in small type, and classified like modern small advertisements. An American journalist Robert Bonner circumvented this restriction in the 1850s by making large advertisements out of the same small advertisement re-peated many times.† The resulting uniform patterning of small print compelled the reader's attention as surely as displayed type. Bonner's innovation was widely copied in both countries. The iteration was often of a single sentence, and sometimes of a single word: both these have many parallels in modern television advertising. But with the raising of the ban on illustration and typographical display, the vogue died out, and it is safe to disregard it as a direct source of iteration in modern copy. All the same, the parallel is illuminating, as the motive that led to its introduction by Bonner may also partly account for its use in modern spoken advertising: the need to overcome the limitation of the medium with respect to the kind of emphasis achieved by large type and display.

---

* Quoted in Sampson (1874), p. 49.
† Presbrey (1929), pp. 236–43.

The period 1850–1910 was one of remarkable expansion in advertising volume, and of the rise of the advertising industry as such. It was a period of stunts and experiments in copywriting and in advertising technique generally: people engaged in the business seemed to be intoxicated by a sense of power and of freedom to create. Among eccentric types of copy which enjoyed temporary popularity was a variation of the 'chameleon technique' whereby an advertisement was passed off as a news item with a glaringly sensational headline. Such fads were short-lived, no doubt because they subordinated other advertising motives to that of attracting attention – and success in this cannot survive widespread imitation.

As the growth of advertising volume continued, there developed a type of copy primarily adapted to providing the consumer with a motive for buying. Perhaps its most influential champion was the American copywriter John E. Powers, who worked by a principle which would be generally accepted today as fundamental to the art of copywriting: 'to say the right things to the right people in an acceptable way'.* This was not just a reaction to the wild, exhibitionist tendency of the times, but a positive step towards the simple and direct style of copywriting now taken for granted. The movement towards a simple, personal, colloquial style in America was followed in Britain by a similar movement, which the rise of the popular press accelerated. Whatever the differences between American and British copy today, the one is certainly not more colloquial or personal (with respect to the consumer) than the other. In fact it is difficult to imagine how either of them could go further in either of these directions.

Disjunctive Language

The disjunctive element of modern advertising language seems to have originated partly in the 'block language' of outdoor displays, and partly in the abbreviated mode of discourse evolved in press advertising.

Although its use in the simplest of naming functions is very old, block language seems to be almost entirely an invention of the printing era. The oldest form of trade-mark, for example, was a discursive sentence: 'X made this sword', etc. or 'X made me' (attributing the power of speech to the artefact). This type of inscription survived into the seventeenth century on products of skilled craftsmanship (for example, musical

---

* Presbrey (1929), p. 306.

instruments). Similarly, commercial publicity was largely conducted in discursive English up to the mid-eighteenth century, despite the great length of sentences incorporating lists of prices and articles for sale. The following, consisting of a single sentence of eighty words, comes from a shopbill Hogarth engraved for his sisters in about 1735:

Mary & Ann Hogarth
from the old Frock Shop the corner of the Long Walk facing the Cloysters, Removed to ye Kings Arms joyning to ye Little Britain gate near Long Walk sells ye best & Most Fashionable Ready Made Frocks, suites Fustian, Ticken & Holland, stript Dimmity & Flanel Wastcoats, blue & canvas Frocks and bluecoat Boys Drapery, Likewise Fustians, Tickens, Hollands, white stript Dimitys, white and stript Flanels in ye piece by Wholesale or Retale, at Reasonable Rates*

In most spheres of communication, block language seems to have developed as a direct consequence of the use of displayed lettering. By spacing, and contrastively prominent typesizes, the general drift of a public announcement can be conveyed to a reader at a glance. The inessentials in small print which serve to connect one main idea to another become redundant through familiarity and convention, and are eventually omitted. What is left is the 'skeleton' of the fully explicit message. The transition from discursive to disjunctive language can be seen clearly in the playbills of the 1750–1850 period. The example shown on p. 172 fills in the gaps between the large print with links such as '. . . To which will be added, for the first Time these Four Years, the favourite Entertainment . . .', which preserve the generally discursive character of the language.

Perhaps superfluous introductory linking passages were often retained out of a feeling for the greater propriety of discursive English, just as gravestone inscriptions today often begin with the communicatively vacuous words 'Here lies . . .'. Discursive English was also used with display typography in nineteenth-century commercial advertising, and was closely allied to another practice now outmoded – that of interlarding the running text of body copy with words and phrases in prominent capitals.

With the expansion of outdoor advertising in the nineteenth century, block language became fully established in display copy, and the railway

* Quoted in Presbrey (1929), p. 32.

Theatre-Royal

For the BENEFIT of
MR JOHN JOHNSTON,
And positively his Last Appearance here this Season.

SATURDAY, July 29. 1815,

Will be presented (by particular Desire of several Ladies and Gentlemen) the Comedy of

The West Indian.

Stockwell, Mr EYRE—Belcour, Mr LACY,
Major O'Flaherty, Mr J. JOHNSTON,
In which Character he will introduce the favourite Song of

The Sprig of Shilelah and Shamrock so Green.

Captain Dudley, Mr ARCHER—Charles Dudley, Mr FINN,—Varland, Mr RUSSELL,
Fulmer, Mr CHIPPENDALE—Stukely, Mr ADCOCK—Sailor, Mr DUFF,
Lady Rusport, Mrs NICOL—Charlotte Rusport, Mrs EYRE——Louisa Dudley, Mrs W. WEST,
Lucy, Miss STANFIELD—Mrs Fulmer, Mrs MOSS.

At the End of the Play, Mr J. JOHNSTON will Sing (in Character) a New Comic Song, written expressly
for him by T. DIBDIN, Esq. describing

A DUEL,

Or, A new Method of taking a long Shot;

With the Death of Mr M'KIRKINCROFT, and the happy Nuptials of

Paddy Whack M'Crack and Miss O'Donoughoo.

To which will be added, for the first Time these Four Years, the favourite Entertainment of

FALSE & TRUE;

Or, the Irishman in Italy.

Count Benini, Mr RUSSELL—The Marchese Caliari, Mr EYRE—Count Florenzi, Mr TRUEMAN,
Leake, Mr W. MURRAY—Thomaso, Mr CHIPPENDALE—Malevoli, Mr FINN—Nicolo, Mr W. WEST,
O'Rafferty, Mr J. JOHNSTON, in which character he will introduce the favourite Comic Song of

" London's the Devil's own Shop,"

Which was received with such unbounded Applause Last Night,

O'RAFFERTY'S CHRISTENING,
And, by particular desire,

" I was the Boy for bewitching 'em ;"

Juliana, Miss STANFIELD—Marchesa, Mrs NICOL—Jaquetta, Mrs W. PENSON.

⁎ On Monday and Tuesday the THEATRE will be closed.

Doors open at Six, to begin precisely at Seven.
Tickets and Places for the Boxes to be had of Mr GARBUTT, at the Box-Office, from Eleven to Three o'clock

stations and street hoardings of the 1870s were covered with posters
bearing such legends as this:

Lloyd's Weekly London News
SALE OVER HALF A MILLION
ONE PENNY

By that time the display methods which had developed for bills and posters were being applied in the press, and something approaching the
modern balance between display copy and body copy in press advertising
was coming into fashion.

Press advertising, however, had developed its own brand of disjunctive
language: an abbreviated mode of discourse which helped the advertiser
to save space and money, just as it does for the small advertiser of today.
But up to the mid-nineteenth century the line between abbreviated and
discursive language was not firmly drawn. Advertisements sometimes
contained what from a modern point of view seems to be a random
mixture of the two modes. In its beginning, abbreviated grammar had
been chiefly confined to oft-repeated formulas such as 'Printed by . . .',
'Tickets to be had from . . .'. It is incidentally in such routine details that
the abbreviated mode is most used in consumer advertising today. Later
it became the custom to use it in a whole advertisement.

After the change-over to display methods in press advertising the
abbreviated mode continued to be used both in headlines and in body
copy, even though the motive for its use, economy of space, no longer
counted in the same way – display headings and illustrations after all
presuppose that an advertiser has room to spare. In fact, the widespread
use of abbreviated language in display advertising in the 1850–1920 era,
and in local display advertising even today, seems to be a case of a linguistic convention outlasting its original usefulness.

Two disjunctive constructions of modern copy appeared in early
newspaper advertisements: the minor clause with initial adjunct (A z)
('For sale, a handsome freehold property . . .'), and the non-finite clause
preceding a minor clause ('To let, desirable residence . . .'; 'Wanted, a
young gentleman of good character . . .'). The initial adjunct or non-
finite clause in such cases was a standard heading or introduction which
told the reader at a glance the purport of the advertisement.

Another special grammatical feature of modern copy, branching clause
parataxis, perhaps grew out of the adaptation of the abbreviated grammar

of press advertising to the new freedom of display lay-out. One kind of abbreviated construction common in nineteenth-century advertising was a finite or non-finite clause with no subject, used where the implied notional subject was the product advertised. (This still occurs on cartons and packages of manufactured substances: 'Dries in less than half an hour'; 'Keeps indefinitely in dry place'.) Under an illustration and a large heading 'Nubian Blacking' in an advertisement of 1885 appears the following body copy:

> Gives a brilliant polish for a week through wet or dry weather. Applied with sponge attached to the cork. Does not injure leather nor clothing.

A second example (dating from 1914) has the heading 'The Mexican Hair Renewer':

> **Prevents** the Hair from falling off.
>
> **Restores** Grey or White Hair to its **Original Colour.**
>
> **Is not a Dye.**

It is easy to see how ignoring the typographical distinction between headline and body copy could lead to a reinterpretation of this text as a single sentence with branching clause parataxis: 'The Mexican Hair Renewer prevents the hair from falling off. Restores grey or white hair to its original colour. Is not a dye'.

Chapter 20

Creative Writing

No word is more often on the lips of the advertising specialist than 'creative'. He 'works creatively' on 'creative campaigns'; when he is not engaged in 'creative planning', he is thinking up 'creative ideas'. Most of this book has been devoted to the normative, *un*creative aspect of advertising language, so it is only proper that we should now turn our attention to the other side of the picture. However, I must confess that I am about to use this word in a rather attenuated sense, just as the advertising world tends to use it in a rather loose and inflated sense. What a copywriter means, if he calls his job creative, is that the preparation of advertising material calls not only for experience and good judgement, but imagination: the imagination by which advertising 'ideas' are conceived in the first place, and by which they are later transformed into the tangible signals of speech, writing, and pictorial communication. I have it in mind to discuss only the ways in which he can be said to make creative use of his linguistic vehicle of communication, the English language.

What does being creative with language mean? It is helpful, in seeking an answer to this, to turn to a variety of language which is creative in its very nature: the language of poetic and prose literature. Poetic licence, or taking liberties with language, is an acknowledged hallmark of literary writing. We might go so far as to say that breaking the rules and conventions of linguistic usage is a necessary condition of literary achievement. The rules and conventions limit the means of expression, and therefore the range of ideas, emotions, and experiences that can be expressed. In order to extend the world of experience, the literary artist has to open up new pathways of communication. There are other means, too, by which poets manipulate language to tap communicative resources not available in its day-to-day utilitarian functions. One is the exploitation of multiple meaning and homonymy: two ways in which language permits of ambiguous interpretation. Another is the introduction of special patterns of regularity into language: rhyme, alliteration, parallelism, and so on. All these topics will be considered with reference to advertising language in this and the following chapter.

Copywriter's Licence

The expression 'poetic licence' somehow suggests that the poet alone has the prerogative of violating the rules of his native tongue. But this is far from true: violations commonly occur (both intentionally and unintentionally) in ordinary conversation. 'Wit' is a term signifying those intentional deviations which are particularly apt and clever, but much more common is a humbler kind of improvisation which amounts to playing with language simply for the fun of it. A friend saw me carrying a book of Bach's *Klavierübung* ('keyboard exercise'), and remarked (referring to the difficulty of the pieces) that they were 'not very übungy'. This, for some reason, was a smiling matter which helped the conversation along. The attachment of an English affix to a German noun had no further point than that of playful indulgence in a linguistic impropriety. In this sense, at least, we all use language creatively. And the kind of violation which occurs in advertising is often more akin to this than to a literary violation. A headline in an advertisement for flights to Mexico in fact contained a very similar device: '¡Sooner than mañana!'. Here the impropriety consisted in using Spanish punctuation and a Spanish word in an advertisement which was otherwise in English.

One might hesitate to apply the word 'creative' in these cases, where the deviant feature apparently has little communicative value. Surely the minimum condition of creativeness is the *constructive* use of violation, whereby some special kind of effect is conveyed. However, what is considered constructive depends on the nature of the linguistic activity. The examples cited above at least had a mild entertainment value; and a linguistic anomaly which contributes to the selling power of advertisement may be considered just as creative, in its own terms, as one which has an artistic function. In fact linguistic violations have more important effects than entertainment in advertising. They can arrest the consumer's attention, and help to imprint the message on his memory. They can also act more subtly, in establishing symbolic connections between the product and the ideals and emotive urges of the consumer. In this last respect, copywriting perhaps comes closest to 'creative writing' in a literary sense.

The number of possible linguistic violations is unlimited, since any rule of language can be violated in any number of different ways. We may start with some examples of violations at various levels of linguistic patterning.

Orthographic

Breaking orthographic rules is a popular practice in trade names, where
the purpose is to provide the product with a distinctive written sym-
bolisation (which may also do duty as its trade-mark). In the names
Brylcreem and *Rice Krispies*, the elements *-creem* and *Krisp-* are clearly
derived, by 'misspelling', from the English words *cream* and *crisp*. Other
familiar examples are (*Jellymeat*) *Whiskas*, the *Ry-* of *Ryvita* and the *Glo-*
of *Glo-coat*. By this device, brand-names get a unique orthographic
image, and yet retain the advantage of being composed of meaningful
linguistic elements. Other violations affect not particular spellings, but
rather the general rules of English orthography. *ScotTowels*, for example,
breaks a rule that capital letters do not occur in the middle of a word,
with small letters on either side. Another device which has been so well
used as to be no longer remarkable is the use of small letters where
capitals would be appropriate. This may extend beyond trade names to
headlines, and indeed to whole advertisements.

Grammatical

Grammatical violations are not usually of the kind which would immediately strike the reader as 'bad grammar'. The following jingles contain
violations which are relatively unobtrusive, because they occur in 'deep
grammar'; that is, they consist in a 'wrong' choice in secondary systems
which are recognised in a relatively refined stage of grammatical analysis.

> Only two Alka-Seltzers ago
> You were feeling downhearted and low.
> Who would ever know you were under the weather
> Only two Alka-Seltzers ago?

> If you're a jelly addict
> Or even if you aren't,
> You'll find that Chivers satisfy
> Like other jellies can't.

The violations occur in the last lines of each. In the first case, *Alka-Seltzer*,
a proper name, is used in a position where only nouns denoting periods
of time (*minutes, weeks, years*, etc.) are strictly acceptable. In the second,
'Like other jellies can't' offends against the rule that comparative clauses
do not have a negative verbal group: it is classed as ungrammatical on
the same grounds that apply to 'I don't like him any more than you
don't', or 'Tom is as friendly as Susie isn't'.

Lexical

The most obvious kind of lexical violation is neologism, or the invention of new lexical items. In Chapter 15 we saw how a certain degree of licence in this respect is a property of the advertising register as a whole, at least as regards adjective compounds. And in general, 'violation' is perhaps too harsh a word to use, since neologism within certain limits is a recognised way of augmenting the resources of the language. The type of neologism we can fittingly note here is a 'nonce' formation which strikes the reader or listener as odd and beyond the customary process of word-formation, because it would be inconceivable that such an item would have any general usefulness in the language. Thus *peelability* (in 'It's got peelability', in reference to an orange) is not the sort of quality one would normally have occasion to mention, in talking about oranges or anything else. Items which share this element of surprise in varying degrees are: 'They're *temptational*'; 'the chocolates that *outsparkle* them all'; '*unzipp* a banana' (combining neologism with 'misspelling'); 'outdoor *biteables*'. More audacious tendencies in neologism are illustrated in 'the *orangemostest* drink in the whole world' and '*Ricicles* are *twicicles* as *nicicles*'. In *orangemostest*, lexical deviation is accompanied by morphological deviation. In the latter example, the words *twicicles* and *nicicles*, like the trade name *Ricicles* itself, are formed on a derivational pattern known as BLENDING: a formation using non-morphemic parts of other words. In this case the non-morphemic constituent is -*icles*, which has apparently been attached to *Rice*, *twice*, and *nice* on the analogy of *ice* and *icicles*. Neither of these examples is from direct address advertising: they occur in the speech of cartoon characters, where a copywriter can exercise a wilder vein of linguistic invention. A special class of neologisms consists of words and compounds formed by combining brand-names with other constituents: *Miliumise*, *Schweppervescence* (another case of blending), *Knorr-fresh*, *Lux-care*.

A second kind of lexical deviation is an unorthodox combination, or collocation, of lexical items, exemplified by 'eat hard' in the following piece of copy:

> Children of today play hard – and they need to eat hard, too. Give them New Zealand Cheddar Cheese – a good body-building food for stamina.

Hard is an adverb which customarily collocates with only a few verbs: 'work hard,' 'try hard', 'run hard', etc. In this sentence it collocates separately with *play* and *eat*. Whereas 'play hard' is not too unusual, being related by antonymy to 'work hard', 'eat hard' is definitely an anomalous collocation, which serves here to reinforce the parallelism between playing and eating.

Semantic

Any infringement of the semantic code of a language is, by the standard of normal communicative functions, 'a piece of nonsense'. This does not necessarily mean that it will communicate nothing: in some kinds of discourse (especially poetry) semantic violations, like paradox and contradiction, play an important role. But in these cases a reader has to find some mode of interpretation which will reconcile a seeming incompatibility of meaning.

In the best circles washing machine is pronounced Parnall.

The peculiarity of the headline lies in a 'misuse' of the word *pronounce*. In any clause of the form 'x is pronounced y', x and y should have a strong phonological resemblance. 'In Germany, "Berlin" is pronounced "Berleen"' makes sense, whether it is true or not. But the above example is analogous to 'In Cornwall, "tree" is pronounced "bush"', a statement which is not only false, but necessarily so. Such absurdities would be objectionable in discourse of a purely informative nature, but here the illogicality is evidently calculated. It catches the attention of the reader, and figuratively makes the point that Parnall is the only kind of washing machine people 'in the best circles' take notice of.

Contextual

Role borrowing, discussed on pp. 99–101, is a type of contextual violation: a use of language in a situation to which it is inappropriate. (As with 'nonsense' and 'absurdity', we understand 'inappropriate' by reference to linguistic rules and conventions, not implying that a violation of these is 'bad' in any sense whatever.) Role borrowing is not necessarily sustained throughout a whole advertisement. In the following case, it is only the opening phrase which strikes a discordant note:

Once upon a time, *this* pretty girl had dry, unmanageable hair – but then she discovered Bristow's Lanolin Shampoo . . .

This television commercial begins with a formula which is appropriate to the start not of an advertisement, but of a fairy tale. Possibly it has the effect of putting the audience in a suitably receptive state of mind: 'Oh yes, we're going to be told a story'. Role borrowing is a versatile device, which can be put to any number of different purposes; some of them were illustrated in Chapter 10. A similar device in which advertising practitioners occasionally indulge for the sake of entertainment value is the game of self-parody – essentially a reproduction and exaggeration of some of the typical features (including linguistic features) of the advertising situation.

A different kind of contextual incongruity is produced by the following headline at the beginning of an advertisement for cheese: '. . . Plus cheese to make a meal of it'. The word *plus*, whether considered a conjunction or a preposition, is a member of a class of words which act as a link between equivalent units. It cannot reasonably occur as the first word in a text. In this case, however, the improbable does happen, and we have to imagine the headline as a continuation of an imaginary sentence. We have to supply both a linguistic and a non-linguistic context, and any context which has to do with a menu will fit. The force of the headline might be expressed: 'whatever you happen to be eating, you can add cheese to make a meal of it'.

This example serves as an introduction to a phenomenon I shall call IMPLICATION OF CONTEXT. When a piece of language is somehow at odds with the situation in which it occurs, one way to make sense of it is to invent a situation (that is, a secondary situation) to which it would be appropriate. This is the kind of act of the imagination we have to make with many lyrical poems. When Shelley begins a poem 'I arise from dreams of thee', or when Byron begins one 'She walks in beauty like the night', the reader is forced to ask such questions as 'who are the "I" and "you", who is the "she" referred to?'. These pronouns have no contextually determined referents; the poet seems to assume that we have already been introduced to them. This is exactly parallel to a way in which advertising copy often makes reference to secondary participants:

> His first toy train is a Hornby train. Big, strong engine. Bright, shiny coaches. His Hornby clockwork set – at only 27/6.

The video of this commercial shows a boy playing with a train set, so in a sense the reference of *his* is given by the secondary situation. But the assumption of prior introduction is still there: it is not as if the commentary had begun '*This boy's* first train is a Hornby train'.

A case where the reference of *he* does not appear in the given secondary situation is a press advertisement headed by two illustrations side by side:

the first shows a yacht and bears the caption 'His sport'; the second shows a bottle of Black & White Whisky, and bears the caption 'His drink'. The body copy goes on to tell us more about this hypothetical 'he':

His world . . . challenging, unpredictable. Where experience is worth a thousand good intentions. So is it with his whisky. It takes many years to perfect the separate arts of distilling, maturing and blending. To produce a whisky as distinctive and consistently fine as Black & White.

In this case our imagination has to do more work: from the information given ('his sport', 'his drink', and 'his world'), we construct a general picture of what the unidentified hero of the advertisement is like. We supposedly build up a favourable image of the typical consumer of the product, and this in turn contributes favourably to our image of the product itself.

Alternative ways to introduce third person secondary participants are to use an indefinite mode of reference ('Here's *another smoker* getting to know Park Drive Tipped'); to use direct deixis ('Tomorrow – *this man* will buy his first packet of Park Drive'); or to identify by means of a proper name ('Meet *Russel Miller*, Fleet Street Reporter'). The last of these is invariably used for non-fictional participants. With fictional participants, the advantage of using the third person pronoun seems to be that it suggests both particular and general reference at the same time: the *he* evokes a kind of Everyman representing the whole class of consumers who fit the role of the secondary participant in the advertisement. This equivocal quality of reference is especially evident in a common use of *he* in the sense of 'the man in your life', as in 'For you – the cool, blue, evocative, dream of a perfume *he*'ll adore'.

Figurative Language

One important omission from the foregoing survey of linguistic unorthodoxies is a discussion of figurative language. That figurative meaning involves an aberrant use of language presupposes an alignment of 'literal' meaning with the orthodox semantic function of words. This is quite justifiable, so long as we exclude from 'figurative language' metaphoric expressions which have passed into everyday use, and have therefore lost their aberrant character. To take a well-known instance:

Some books are to be tasted, others to be swallowed, and some few to be chewed and digested.

This sentence from Bacon's essay 'Of Studies' is plainly a semantic absurdity unless we make the effort to interpret it in a figurative way; that is, to understand *tasted, swallowed, chewed,* and *digested* in an abnormal sense. This, and in fact most cases of metaphor, can be treated as a violation either at the semantic or at the lexical level. Semantically, it consists in an incompatibility of meanings (people do not chew or swallow books); lexically, it is an unorthodox collocation of the verbs *tasted, swallowed,* etc. with the noun *books.* It may seem irreverent to compare this with a sentence from a toothpaste advertisement which again contains an inappropriate collocation of the verb *taste* – this time with an abstract noun, instead of with a noun denoting an inedible object:

What does the tingle taste like?

Asked to give a serious answer to this question, we could but reply 'Tingles do not have taste', indicating the nonsensical, or semantically unacceptable nature of the question.

Metaphors are valuable in advertising language because they can help to suggest the right kind of emotive associations for the product. The way we interpret a metaphor is to see a connection, or symbolic identity, between the literal and figurative meaning of an item. (So, in Bacon's apophthegm, we understand an equation 'books = food'.) Such irrational identifications epitomise in language what in more general terms is meant by building up an 'image' for a product. Or, to put the matter the other way round, a brand image is a 'metaphor' by which a product is identified with an object of the consumer's desires. The relation between metaphor and image-building can be seen in extracts from a campaign for Kellogg's Corn Flakes which had as its theme the equation 'Corn Flakes = sunshine'. The campaign consisted of a series of commercials in which a four-line verse, sung to a guitar accompaniment, was followed by a short piece of commentary. Here is one of the series, showing how collocative clashes ('sugar and sunshine'; 'eat sunshine') express the metaphorical basis of the message:

(Sung):   This little girl knows lots of tricks
          She knows that sugar and sunshine mix
          Add the milk and now you know
          How little girls eat sunshine.

(Spoken): Kellogg's Corn Flakes. That's how you can eat sunshine
          every day. Don't let little things distract you when
          you're eating Corn Flakes.

Here are extracts from other advertisements in the campaign in which *sun* and *sunshine* are used figuratively:

> Here's a man who likes the sun in his garden and in his breakfast plate too.

> Poor old John – he's caught no fish
> But he's caught the sun in his breakfast dish.

> A paper boy's life's an early one
> But Joe can help himself to sun.

> They switch on the sunshine when you want it.

Figurative language also has a striking and memorable quality which suits it for slogans and headlines:

> Benson's bring Bond St. to your home

> Flowers by Interflora speak from the heart

> 'Terylene' keeps its promises

> Wash the big city right out of your hair

> There's a really good meal in a box of eggs

These five examples are metaphorical only in a loose sense. In fact they illustrate varieties of figurative meaning for which traditional rhetoric had other names. The first is an example of SYNECDOCHE: 'Bond St.', an expression of very specific meaning (in fact a proper name) stands for a general concept – fashionable jewellery and luxury goods. The second and third are cases of PERSONIFICATION: flowers are invested with the human faculty of speech, and 'Terylene' with the human ability to make and keep promises. The fourth and fifth examples seem to fit best into the category of METONYMY: 'the big city' and 'a really good meal' are reasonably interpreted as standing for a semantically related concept, which could be expressed 'the dirt of the big city' and 'the ingredients of a really good meal'. The last sentence is not so strikingly figurative as the others; it contains the kind of metonymy which we readily use in day-to-day conversation.

A further type of figurative language is illustrated by these three examples, in which an epithet used in an unusual sense is italicised:

> *Sophisticated*, sweet-to-drink Pink Lady.

Soft, enchanting, *smiling* colour – that's the
gift of Focus to your hair.

Feel its slim, *purposeful* shape in your hand.

These appear in advertisements (for a drink, a hair cosmetic, and a cigarette
lighter) which emphasise the glamour and imaginative appeal of the product. The violation in each case seems to meet the condition of personification, in that an adjective expressing a human attribute is attached to an
impersonal head. But the effect is not to make us imagine what is denoted
by the head as a living thing. Indeed, it is difficult to describe what the
effect is, or to attach any sense to a phrase like 'purposeful shape'. Perhaps
we might interpret the adjective as somehow applying to the user of the
product, rather than the product itself. Here figurative language communicates only at a level of fantasy and suggestion.

Ambiguity

Ambiguity can be defined, in linguistic description, as a many-one
relationship between levels, whereby different meanings are expressed
alike in form (MULTIPLE MEANING), or different formal items have the same
spelling or pronunciation (HOMONYMY). Dictionaries of English afford
thousands of illustrations of these phenomena. Thus *stern* as an adjective
and *stern* as a noun are homonyms; the adjective *thin* has more than one
meaning, as can be seen by the fact that it can be an antonym either of
thick or of *fat*.

Homonymy and multiple meaning tend to be thought of in connection
with lexis, rather than grammar. But a very familiar example of
homonymy in advertising is grammatical: the slogan 'Players please' can
be read either as a polite request 'Please give me some Players', or as a
statement that Players are pleasing. As is often the case in advertising, this
ambiguity hinges on orthography rather than pronunciation: in reading
the sentence aloud, we are forced to indicate by intonation one or other of
the two interpretations.

In informative or reasoned discourse, ambiguity is usually considered a
fault to be eliminated. In poetry, on the contrary, it is usually treated as a
means of enriching the communicative resources of the language, by a
superimposition or juxtaposition of alternative interpretations. As with
violations, this deliberate exploitation of ambiguity is not just a feature of
literary language, but of any situation (for example, private talk) in which
the inventive or imaginative use of language is socially allowable. A pun

or play on words can serve a serious literary purpose, or it may simply provoke amusement, or add spice to an unpretentious conversational exchange.

A common type of play on ambiguity in advertising is one which involves interpreting an item both as part of an idiom and as a lexical item in its own right:

> When the wind has a bite – and you feel like a bite – then bite on a Whole Nut.

Here, the first two occurrences of *bite* belong to special idioms, whereas in the third repetition it has its usual verbal meaning. Another example is the slogan 'Suck it and Vitamin C', which depends for its point on the homonymy of *C* and the verb *see*. In this case, the item is not repeated, but the two interpretations are 'superimposed' on the same occurrence of it.

Puns on brand-names are also popular. In this jingle, use is made of *nuts* in its primary meaning, *nuts* meaning 'crazy', and *Nux* as the name of the product:

> You'll go nuts for the nuts you get in Nux
> It fills you up and gives you lots of go.

Much of the following television commentary revolves round the ambiguity of *Superfine* as a brand-name and *superfine* as an adjective meaning 'extra specially good':

> A delicious gingerbread man for Tommy, baked with loving care. Ooops! And Pam's favourite chocolate cake. She's a superfine mum and a superfine cook. She chooses Kraft Superfine Margarine. It creams thoroughly, instantly. Gives perfect textured cakes always. And Kraft Superfine is made from the purest vegetable oils. For superfine mums, and cooks. There's only one quality margarine – Kraft Superfine.

The same device is used in this commercial for Nimble Bread:

> She's the nimblest girl around. Nimble is the way she goes. Nimble is the bread she eats. Light, delicious, Nimble.

The brand-name bears the right kind of association for an energy-giving food, and the pun underlines this association, by reinforcing it with the use of the word *nimble* in its accustomed sense.

Chapter 21

Rhyme and Rhetoric

If a copywriter wished to claim ancient and noble ancestry for his profession, he might, with some justification, see himself in the tradition of persuasive oratory going back to the orators of ancient Greece and Rome. The art of effective speaking and writing, codified in manuals of rhetoric, has been an important part of curricula of liberal education through the ages. Its influence lives today in the handbooks of composition and usage, with their lists of figures of speech – a remnant of the more compendious catalogues of classical rhetoric.

We have seen how at least some rhetorical figures, particularly those involving semantic violations, such as metaphor and metonymy, have found a place in the repertoire of copywriting. But we have yet to examine an important class of rhetorical effects which depend on a repetition of linguistic patterns, for example parallelism (repetition of formal patterns) and alliteration (repetition of initial consonants or consonant features). Since the art of rhetoric has always been closely connected with the art of poetic composition, this class of repetitive effects can be extended to include those which play a part in conventions of versification. Metre is a pattern composed of rhythm groups (feet) consisting of similar or identical patterns of stressed and unstressed syllables; rhyme is a pattern of 'identity of sound between words or verse-lines extending from the end to the last fully accented vowel and not further'.*

It is only the verse conventions of modern European culture that give rhyme and metre a special status. They are not, and never have been, restricted to verse, and in other cultures not these, but other patterns of repetition have been basic components of versification: parallelism in the Hebrew psalms; alliteration in old Germanic poetry. Linguistically then, all these and other similar phenomena can be placed in the same general category, to which I shall give the name SCHEMES.

A scheme is definable as a correspondence or partial identity (over and above the degree of identity inherent in language structure) between

---

* Definition in the Concise Oxford Dictionary.

equivalent pieces of text in proximity. By stipulating *partial* identity, I
exclude exact repetitions characteristic of television advertising:

> Best fish – all fish – guaranteed boneless.
> Best fish – all fish – guaranteed boneless.
> Findus Fish Sticks – the best you can buy.

These might, however, be considered special cases of schematic patterning: those which fulfil the condition of identity to the greatest possible degree. In part of a jingle advertising Smarties, the identity is not
exact – each of the four clauses beginning 'Wot a lot' differs from the
others in at least one word:

> Wot a lot you get
> Wot a lot I got
> Wot a lot we got
> Wot a lot of fun you get
> When you ask for a tube of Smarties.

Language in its very nature consists in a successivity of partially identical
events, which are abstracted as units at various levels and ranks, so the
definition of schemes necessarily stipulates that the degree of regularity
should be greater than that which is characteristic of language in general.
This means identity of secondary structures, and identity of items within
structures (for example, the repeated sequence 'Wot a lot' in the Smarties
commercial). In the following case, no single item is actually repeated, but
there is an exact correspondence of secondary structures (E H):

> Fine workmanship
> Beautiful design
> Real compactness
> Wonderful value

This is quite a strong parallelism, in view of the vast structural variation
possible in the English noun group.

Phonological Schemes

As everyone knows, alliteration is a device widely used in advertising
slogans:

> Give me Gordon's – everytime
>
> E*l*ectro*l*ux brings *l*uxury to *l*ife
>
> *B*uilt *B*etter by *B*urco for you

It is also sometimes a feature of product names: 'Fison's Fairway', 'Morris Mini-Minor', 'Kellogg's Corn Flakes'. In some cases, it is even sustained through a whole advertisement, as in the case of the alliterated *f*s of this commercial:

(Spoken): Eskimo! For fuller flavour fish . . . fresher fillets . . . tastier fishcakes . . . and now – *new* from Eskimo . . . delicious chunky fishsteaks! Ready-cooked . . . a man-sized meal in a moment! Eskimo fishsteaks are all fish . . . man-sized . . . chunky . . . full of that fresh sea flavour! Give your family fuller flavour fishsteaks from Eskimo!

(Sung):   Go go go go for Eskimo
            The frozen food with the fuller flavour.

(Whispered): Eskimo!

Rhyme is, of course, commonly found in jingles. But it is also, like alliteration, a device which helps to make headlines and slogans striking and easy to remember:

A t*oast* to the h*ost*

Don't be v*ague* – ask for H*aig*

Go to t*own* with Cr*own* wallpapers

Sh*ave* and s*ave* with Erasmic

gr*ace* . . . sp*ace* . . . p*ace*

The last example is a series of headlines accompanying illustrations in a Jaguar car advertisement.

A less obvious type of scheme is vowel harmony, which here takes the form of a repetition of the same vowel in successive stressed syllables: 'Mum Rollette protects you best'. This example also has a rhythmic regularity, illustrating that metre, like rhyme, is not confined to versified advertising. It has a perfectly regular trochaic pattern, with two syllables in each foot except the last:

$$/ \quad \times / \quad / \quad \times / \quad / \quad \times / \quad /$$
Mum Roll/ette pro/tects you/ best.

It is surprising how often slogans and other key parts of an advertising message evince some kind of rhythmic regularity. Effects like rhyme and alliteration shout at us, but a metrical scheme may easily pass unnoticed, although when it is brought to our attention, we see that it contributes to the schematic 'neatness' of the whole passage. For example, a kind of metre underlies one of the slogans already quoted: 'Don't be vague – ask for Haig'.

It is probably oversimplifying matters to say that phonological schemes help to make striking and memorable pieces of language. There is an undefined 'ritualistic' quality about them which makes people want to repeat them, and this seems to be at least partially what is involved when a slogan 'catches on' with the general public. Of course, this is not just a property of advertising slogans; such schemes are also common in political slogans, and catch phrases of all types.* It may be an indication of the fundamental nature of their appeal that they can be perceived even by people who are not familiar with the language in which the message is composed.

Perhaps this mysterious and often sub-conscious effect on the listener accounts for a use of phonological schemes in television advertising in parts of the message where memorability is not especially important:

> Bubbly Stergene, soft – gentle – safe – essential for all your finest things.

On a first impression, the order of the adjectives *soft*, *gentle*, *safe*, and *essential* in this passage might appear to be random and unconsidered. But in fact it conceals a rather involved combination of schemes, including alternating alliteration and vowel harmony. *Soft* and *safe* go together as monosyllables with an initial *s*; *gentle* and *essential* go together as polysyllables having a short *e* sound followed by *n* in their stressed vowel, and a final syllabic *l*. These words are spoken slowly and deliberately against a soft musical background: their effect on the ear is seductively hypnotic.

Rhyme, alliteration, and vowel harmony generally take the form of a partial repetition of a stressed syllable. Other variations of this general type of patterning are a congruence of both initial consonant and vowel, as in 'Match it with a Matinee', and a repetition of a whole stressed syllable, as in 'A man's at his best with a Manikin'. There are numerous kinds of phonological scheme, apart from those for which names are available.

---

* In this connection, see Roman Jakobson's analysis of the political slogan 'I like Ike' in Sebeok (1960), p. 357.

Formal Schemes

Formal schemes, or parallelisms, are often 'rhetorical' in a familiar sense of the word, in that they heighten the emotional tone of the message, giving insistent emphasis to points of strategic importance. The following series of display headings coincides with a parallelism of clauses beginning with 'It's . . .'.

> It's new!
> It's crisper!
> It's lighter!
> It's the
> New Ryvita

Building up to a climax by a sequence of clauses which begin in the same way is a commonplace device of popular oratory. In advertising, typography often contributes to the impact of the parallelism. In the original of this example, each line of the series was printed in a different colour, and the final line containing the brand-name was printed in bigger type. Special features of display also reinforce parallelism in the following portion of an advertisement for Halex toothbrushes:

Strong blue inner tufts to   Soft white outer tufts to
clean teeth   massage gums

These two headings balance one another side by side under the headline 'Get a Halex twin for double protection'.

In body copy, too, parallelism can be supported by lay-out:

> New suspension gives even better comfort and handling
> New four-speed gearbox with overdrive or Borg-Warner
>   Automatic as optional extras
> New super-luxury trim
> New braking system
> New fully reclining seats

In the majority of cases, as in this one, the scheme coincides with a paratactic structure enumerating points in favour of the product. This is also its main function in television advertising, where the segments of the pattern, instead of coinciding with visual correspondences of lay-out, often synchronise with changes in the film sequence.

Today . . . the best-selling soft toilet tissue is Andrex . . . Why? Andrex is soft, Andrex is strong, Andrex has five colours, Andrex

sells best – because it's better. Better for you. Better for your family.
Get Andrex tomorrow.

Each clause beginning with *Andrex* in this script acts as a 'caption' to a
new stage in the visual sequence. The parallelism 'Better for you. Better
for your family', on the other hand, has no special relation with the video.
   Further, parallelism is sometimes used to underline a contrast:

> Remember 'Marzine'
> Forget travel sickness

> The shine sealed in – the dirt sealed out

To this kind of figure the name 'antithesis' is usually applied.

The Combination of Phonological and Formal Schemes

Two examples given earlier in this chapter illustrate how phonological
and formal schemes may coincide with one another. In the Smarties
jingle quoted on p. 187, the repeated phrase 'Wot a lot', beside being part of
a parallelism, contains the rhyme of 'Wot' and 'lot' (emphasised by deviant
spelling). In the Eskimo commercial on p. 188, the concluding line of the
jingle, 'The frozen fish with the fuller flavour', also has a minor parallelism (the repetition of the pattern '*the* + adjective + noun' in both the
main and the embedded noun group), and this is accompanied by
alliteration on each combination of adjective and noun. In addition, there
is a slight metrical reinforcement of the parallelism, in that a foot of two
syllables ($/ \times$) occurs on each adjective. This shows how an unsuspected
degree of schematic regularity can underlie what is on the face of it a
straight-forward slogan. It should not be assumed that such effects are
necessarily difficult to achieve. In general, a closely-knit schematic pattern,
in which a regularity at one level coincides with one at another, requires
little subtlety either from the writer or the audience. But then subtlety
is not generally what the copywriter is aiming at.
   There is a type of television commercial which is schematic throughout,
both formally and phonologically. In this one, the repeated switches
from the spoken commentary to a sung refrain are part of an almost
liturgical design, in which repetitions of visual sequences harmonise with
the organisation of the verbal message:

(Sung):   Fruits by Del Monte

(Spoken): Fruits with top-of-the-tree flavour. That's the Del Monte
           difference. Enjoy these luxurious fruits. Luscious peaches –

(Sung):   with the difference that's Del Monte.

(Spoken): Delicious pears –

(Sung):   with the difference that's Del Monte.

(Spoken): Delectable pineapple –

(Sung):   with the difference that's Del Monte

(Spoken): Look for the tins with the Del Monte shield.

On the formal level, there is the threefold repetition of the sung refrain, together with the parallelism of the preceding noun groups 'Luscious peaches', 'Delicious pears', and 'Delectable pineapple', each having the structure E H. Then there is the alliterative connection between *difference* and *Del Monte*, repeated four times in the advertisement. Other alliterations are the repeated *t* of 'top-of-the-tree flavour' and the alternating *d*s and *p*s of 'Delicious pears' and 'Delectable pineapple'. The initial consonance of *delicious* and *delectable* might be taken as part of a chain of phonological connections between the four adjectives *luxurious, luscious, delicious, delectable*. But perhaps this is taking the search for schemes beyond what would be perceived by a viewer on a single hearing.

Jingles

The place to look for schematic patterning above all is the television jingle. This is, of course, partly because jingles are written for music, which in itself demands some kind of rhythmic regularity. But not all jingles adhere to a rigid verse pattern. Some, especially those sung to a fast jazz tempo, are rhythmically almost indistinguishable from ordinary speech:

> What a happy thought,
> Hey, Mabel!
> Great idea,
> Black Label.
> Nothing's too good for good company
> Carling's Black Label's here.
> Yes, Carling's Black Label sparkling, bright and clear.
> Hey, Mabel!
> Black Label!

At the other extreme, there are jingles which are not only metrical, but highly schematic in other respects:

Lucky Numbers, Lucky Numbers,
Chocolate 'n chew.
You'll be lucky, mighty lucky
I'm lucky too!
Bite that chewy chocolate
That's lucky for you.
Take your pick and you're in luck with
Sweet Seventeen
Chew that chewy Cherry White –
You see what I mean?
Caramello, Lemon Log,
Lucky Fifteen!

      . . . . . .

Wipe it on, Windolene
Wipe it on, Windolene
That's how to get your windows clean.
Wipe it off straight away
Wipe it off, no delay
So easy with New Windolene.
Windolene.

Such density of schemes and repetitions is not uncommon in traditional
ballads and modern pop songs. But perhaps a more fitting analogy,
bringing out the ritualistic aspect of advertising jingles, is with children's
games and nursery rhymes.

Chapter 22

Non-standard Advertising Language

This final chapter will illustrate some less usual types of advertising copy. 'Standard advertising English' is what is expected and normal in the advertising situation. But there is always a premium on originality of approach, and copywriters are always looking out for new ways of approaching the consumer, and for new means of expression. Out of this tendency have arisen in recent years styles of advertising copy for which certain descriptive adjectives come to mind: the 'jazz style', the 'whimsy style', the 'zany style', and so forth. These styles embody linguistic unorthodoxy in two respects: in the first place, they are marked by an avoidance of various hackneyed features of 'standard' copy; secondly, some of them are distinguished by a liberal use of schemes and violations. 'Style' is the most appropriate word to use, for they tend to be associated with special types of audience, and to suggest a special tone of address. They are often found in 'quality' magazines and newspapers, where, it appears, the straight-forward and often aggressive tactics of popular press and television advertising are out of place, and a more sophisticated approach to the consumer is desirable.)

Terseness and Understatement

We start with one of the milder types of unconventionality. Here are two examples of the 'clipped style', in which direct address copy perhaps comes closest to understatement:

> BP Visco-static **Longlife** is different. It's compounded in a new way so it can take any engine dirt particles, sticky as toffee apples, and wrap them up. Seals them away. Keeps them harmless. So BP **Longlife** assures cleaner engine protection over longer mileage. And that's why you can now double your normal mileage between oil changes . . . Reassuring, isn't it?

> Eggs go into it. And best dairy butter. With lemons, sugar, milk, a pinch of salt, and nothing else. Nothing to spoil the true tingling

taste of **real** lemon cheese as only Moorhouses can make it. Most people who have tried it agree it's the creamiest purest lemon spread you can buy. See what **you** think.

Although they contain many conventional advertising features, these advertisements (from *The Observer Colour Supplement* and *Women's Own* respectively) convey a certain difference in attitude: 'We know our product is good – we don't need to shout it from the roof-tops. But we'd advise you to try it, all the same'. There is no direct exhortation to buy; the only imperative in both pieces is the final clause of the second, 'See what **you** think', which is merely an invitation to confirm the advertiser's own high opinion of his product. In place of a final imperative in the first example is the remark 'Reassuring, isn't it?', which seems to assume that the consumer cannot fail to agree with the writer. The reason for calling this type of copy 'clipped' is that it abounds in short sentences, which keep the tone of appeal in a 'low key', and seem symptomatic of a refusal to rhapsodise about the product. The effect of a casual, terse, manner of address is aided by prosiopesis in the first example: 'Seals them away. Keeps them harmless'. The eulogistic element is controlled, with an emphasis on authenticity; *real* and *true* are adjectives in the first passage. Where the copywriter does revert to conventional advertising hyperbole is in the intensified superlative expression 'the creamiest purest lemon spread you can buy'. But even this is toned down by the preceding qualification 'Most people who have tried it agree . . .', which is unusually modest in that it admits that *some* people may *dis*agree. In both cases, the writer seems to say 'We don't have to clothe our message in fair words; we just state, as simply as possible, what our product is'.

The tendency to use short sentences is even stronger in the next two specimens, in which terseness does not so much suggest plain speaking, as contribute to a streamlined, anti-romantic style of 'mood' appeal:

Wallpapers. By the million. By Crown. Incredible variety, selection, range, choice. Choice. That's the word. No other wallpapers give such choice. Patterns. Textures. Finishes. Colours. Styles. Prices. Everything. Wallpapers for the 'with-its'. For the 'trads'. For the mood-makers. For the colour-schemers. For the budget-buyers. Wallpapers for everyone. Ad infinitum. For every place, every purpose. Whatever you want from a wallpaper you get it from Crown.

24 big, big curvers give you this look. Curvers invented by Toni. A cross between a roller and a curler. Works like a roller. No curls, just

curves. Lasts like a curler. For ages. Curver lotion makes it last. Perms-
in the curve. All come in a big, new box. To give you a new, new
look. Uncurly. Smooth'n Sleek. Get the look for 15 shillings. It's the
best 15 shillings you'll ever spend on your hair.

These, like the previous examples, avoid the brashness of conventional
sales talk, and are restrained in the use of commendatory adjectives. But
they also contain schemes and word play. These extra features seem to
add animation to the language, imparting a racy, hyper-modern image of
the product. There is extensive parallelism in the first example (for
instance, the series of groups beginning 'For the . . .'), and a pun in the
invented compound 'colour-schemers'. The second example contains
phonological schemes ('No curls, just curves'; 'Smooth 'n Sleek') and
several examples of prosiopesis. It is very difficult to characterise the
appeal made by these advertisements, except by an intuitively felt analogy
to the machinelike rhythms and emotive understatement of a popular
jazz idiom.

This analogy gains some support from the next quotation, from a
thirty-second commercial script in which the commentary is accompanied
by 'music . . . with dominant beat':

> Get this different tasting Sparkling Tango. Tell you why: made
> from whole oranges. Taste those oranges. Taste the tang in Tango.
> Tingling tang, bubbles – sparkles. You drink it straight. Goes down
> great. Taste the tang in Tango. New Sparkling Tango.

This shares features observed in the other examples: very short sentences,
phonological schemes (especially alliteration) and prosiopesis.

Masculine and Feminine Styles

Although three of the preceding pieces of copy have been from women's
magazines, the 'clipped' and 'jazz' styles, with their rather subdued tone,
might be thought especially suitable to a male audience. Men are inclined
to dislike extravagant language and attempts to play on the feelings. Also
the 'debunking' attitude to advertising is more highly developed in men
than in women. As an example of an emotional appeal to men, the following body copy from an advertisement in *Punch* combines the characteristics of both styles:

> Lights, flights. Rains and trains. Daily papers, ticker-tapers. Always
> tearing, life's so wearing. So step back. Relax. A good pipe. A tin

of Four Square. You'll soon find contentment. In a slow-burning, cool-smoking, naturally-matured tobacco. A perfect tobacco. A tobacco with a teasing flavour. And a choice of seven subtly distinct blends. To soothe you and smooth you and give you a truly enjoyable smoke, Four Square. You'll like it.

The most used phonological scheme is rhyme (*lights/flights*, *tearing/wearing*, etc.). Phonological schemes blend with parallelism in 'A perfect tobacco. A tobacco with a teasing flavour' and 'To soothe you and smooth you'. This advertisement promises an emotional state (relaxation) rather than any tangible benefits. But it manages to convey the promise in a tone of man-to-man frankness. Praise of the product is of a 'no-nonsense' kind ('A perfect tobacco'; 'a truly enjoyable smoke'), and the final claim 'You'll like it' is disarmingly modest.

After a sample of masculine understatement, we turn to the gushing hyperbole of the 'whimsy style' sometimes used in addressing a female audience. The following are two sections of an advertisement in *Woman's Own*:

> Preparing sandwiches at the last minute may ensure they're fresh, but with Food-Saver, you can make them the previous night. By tomorrow they'll lose not a single "M'm" of flavoursome moisture! Wrap them appe-**tightly** – that's the Food-Saver secret.

> Meat gets **so** tired in the fridge. Double-Wrap it tightly in Food-Saver and it stays butchershop-fresh till you're ready to cook it. It doesn't just save – it **safeguards.**

Characteristic of this style is a rather capricious bent in neologism: "*M'm*" as a noun; *double*-wrap as a verb; *flavoursome*; *butchershop-fresh*. Other kinds of linguistic extravagance are also found: *appe-**tightly*** is a blend motivated by word-play. In the following example, also from a women's magazine, much of the word-play and neologism depends on the resemblance between *pie* and *Spry* (the brand-name). The picture shows a pie-crust hovering in mid-air over a cherry pie.

Headline: Why Spry makes the lightest pastry
(But frankly, this picture is pure Spry-in-the-Sky)

Body copy: We made this cherry-pie the other day. And because we made it with Spry, we called it cherry-Spry. At that stage we removed its Spry-crust (shame). And then we took this Spry-in-the-sky picture to show you, symbolically, that Spry makes very, very, very light pastry.

Subhead: Why Spry makes the lightest pastry!
Body copy: Spry has air already whipped into it. And this is what makes
               it so phenomenally easy to mix. (You can whisk it in with a
               fork in 60 seconds.) It's this sheer speed in the mixing that
               makes a Spry-crust so very much nicer than ordinary pie-
               crust.

Subhead: No more tricks – just magic
Body copy: If you use Spry for your pastry, and we strongly recommend
               it, don't expect it to float in mid-air. It won't. (And it'd
               look rather silly if it did.) On the other hand, it will vanish
               very deliciously indeed. Not into thin air. Into happy
               family.

Other odd features of this piece of copy are the deviant collocation
'vanish . . . deliciously'; a final stroke of wit in the 'false' parallelism of
'into thin air' and 'into happy family'; and an almost editorial use of *we*,
apparently referring to the agency personnel rather than to the advertiser.

The 'chic style' of women's fashion advertisements has as its speciality
a wide range of descriptive adjectives and an obscure figurative mode of
expression reflecting the mystique of the fashion world. The phrase
'Fashion future perfect' in this example from *Vogue* makes neither
grammatical nor semantic sense to me, whatever it may convey to a
female mind:

Headline: Fashion future perfect
Body copy: Go for fashion . . . and you go for Mölnlycke (**say it Mern-**
               licker), the dreamiest, dishiest dress fabrics ever. Subtle
               colours reflecting fashion's French Impressionist theme . . .
               enchanting designs that make up oh-so-gorgeous Mölnlycke
               Swedish fabrics . . . cotton and easy-care cotton/synthetic
               blends. Fashion future perfect from leading stores every-
               where.

This style resembles the highly-coloured idiom of fashion features in
women's magazines.

Both the 'whimsy' and 'chic' styles give the impression of woman
speaking to woman, just as the Four Square advertisement gave the impression of man speaking to man. One of the reasons for this is the use of
forms of language which are associated with female speech, for example
the adjective *gorgeous*, and the graphically emphasised *so* of 'Meat gets **so**

tired in the fridge', representing an equivalent intonational emphasis in many women's speech. The prefatory exclamation *oh* of *oh-so-gorgeous* is almost a stylised feature of this sort of advertisement. *Oh-so* is used as if it were a sub-modifier, equivalent to *very*, *really*, etc.

Experimental Styles

The examples given so far are quite conventional compared with some of the odder experiments in copywriting to be seen in our 'better' magazines. The reader can form his own judgment about the motive for, or effect of, the 'zany style' illustrated by this headline and body copy of an advertisement in *Punch*:

Headline: Moral turpitude (BP)

Body copy: Blast the Heath! Highwayman haunted. A holdup hid in every hollybush. Mask and musket: Muffled hoofbeats in the misty moonlight. Travel treacherous: Even if you gained the Spaniards hostelry intact, those pesky stand-and-delivery men gave you no peace. What with that fellow Turpin jackaboxing from trapdoors, rushing down the underground passages. And the stamp champ tramp of stabled Bess.

Mind you, all that popping about was so much poppycock. Even H. Ainsworth Esqr. admits to whitewashing the black villain in 'Rookwood'. Turpin in sad truth was just a butcher's apprentice turned cattle thief, turned small-time Tobyman. Still, although the legendary ride to York never took place, there's no denying Turpin ended up there: Hanged for horse-stealing on April 7th 1739. Nor's there denying that less legendary Highwaymen were, literally, thick as thieves en route. In fact travel wasn't nearly as rosy as fiction oft paints in those olden days – BP. Before Petrol. Today the hazards of the highway are happily halved. You needn't bear a barker in your boot, they serve bitter not bullets at the Spaniards and BP represents everything that's helpful in travel. You'll find they don't half deliver at any BP station from Hampstead to York and all points North, South, East, West.

The schemes, violations, and double meanings in this example are too numerous to mention. It is a type 'literary' copy in which imaginatively unconventional use of language is itself one of the major appeals to the reader's interest.

This does not exhaust a possible list of deviant styles of copywriting, for any copywriter, exercising originality, can invent a special style for a particular advertisement. Consider the peculiarities of the following piece of copy:

Headline: Liquid assets

Body copy: in so many famous breweries and bottleries are the agile Coventry Climax fork lift trucks, able with equal ease, to cope with case or keg, barrel, bottle or cask . . . reducing handling costs and breakages, speeding out-put by faster, more economical loading.
Being admired above are just a few of the well-known labels that start life with a lift from Coventry Climax.

It contains the alliteration and play on words noted in previous styles; also the facetious neologism *bottleries*, coined for the sake of parallelism and alliteration with the preceding *breweries*. But it also contains two occurrences of a special type of clause inversion where the verb *to be* and the subject are, in that order, postponed to the end of the clause: 'Liquid assets in so many famous breweries and bottleries are . . .'; 'Being admired above are . . .'. This inversion belongs to the English of popular journalism, and does not form a recognisable pattern with the other features of the copy. A strange, distinctive, and devious style of language seems to have been brought into being expressly for this advertisement.

The growth of 'off-beat' advertising styles may reflect the increasing thickness of the public's armour of defence against conventional sales language, and the corresponding need of the advertising profession to experiment in new and more sophisticated methods of attack. We might ask whether these tendencies presage the obsolescence of the stale forms of expression enshrined in 'standard advertising English'. I would be inclined to say 'No': 'standard advertising English', however familiar its ring on the ears of the public, embodies universal principles of salesmanship, and these deviant styles derive their power mainly through their 'differentness', which would no longer have its effect if they were used too widely. However, my task in this book has been description, not prediction; the ever developing methods of mass communication will no doubt provide more fields for the investigator of the future.

Bibliography

BARTHES, R. (1963), 'Le Message Publicitaire, Rêve et Poësie', *Cahiers de la Publicité*, pp. 91–6.

DE VOE, M. (1956), *Effective Advertising Copy*. New York.

DIXON, R. M. W. (1964), 'On Formal and Contextual Meaning', *Acta Linguistica*, 14, pp. 23–45.

DUNN, S. W. (1956), *Advertising Copy and Communication*. New York.

ELLIOT, Blanche B. (1962), *A History of English Advertising*. London.

EVANS, B. I. (1955), ed., *Studies in Communication*. London.

FIRTH, J. R. (1957), *Papers in Linguistics*. London.

FLESCH, R. (1951), *How to Test Readability*. New York.

FRIES, C. C. (1952), *The Structure of English*. New York.

GALLIOT, M. (1955), *Essai sur la Langue de la Réclame Contemporaine*. Toulouse.

GIMSON, A. C. (1962), *An Introduction to the Pronunciation of English*. London.

HALLIDAY, M. A. K. (1961), 'Categories of the Theory of Grammar', *Word*, 17. 3, pp. 241–92.

HALLIDAY, M. A. K. (1963a), 'The Tones of English', *Archivum Linguisticum*, 15. 1, pp. 1–28.

HALLIDAY, M. A. K. (1963b), 'Class in Relation to the Axes of Chain and Choice', *Linguistics: an International Review*, 2, pp. 11–15.

HALLIDAY, M. A. K. (1964), 'The Linguistic Study of Literary Texts', in *Proceedings of the IXth International Congress of Linguists*, ed. H. G. Lunt, The Hague, pp. 302–7.

HALLIDAY, M. A. K., McINTOSH, A., and STREVENS, P. (1964), *The Linguistic Sciences and Language Teaching*. London.

HARRIS, R., and SELDON, A. (1962), *Advertising and the Public*. London.

JEFKINS, F. W. (1958), *Copywriting and its Presentation*. London.

JESPERSEN, O. (1909–1947), *A Modern English Grammar on Historical Principles*. London.

JESPERSEN, O. (1924), *Philosophy of Grammar*. London.

JOOS, M. (1962), *The Five Clocks*. Bloomington, Ind.

LEECH, G. N. (1963), 'Disjunctive Grammar in British Television Advertising', *Studia Neophilologica*, 35. 2, pp. 256–64.

LEES, R. B. (1960), *The Grammar of English Nominalizations*. Bloomington, Ind.

LEVIN, S. R. (1962), *Linguistic Structures in Poetry*. The Hague.

McINTOSH, A., and HALLIDAY, M. A. K. (1966), *Patterns of Language*. London.

MARCHAND, H. (1960), *The Categories and Types of Present-Day English Word-Formation*. Wiesbaden.

OGILVY, D. (1964), *Confessions of an Advertising Man*. Paperback edition: Dell Books, New York.

PACKARD, V. (1957), *The Hidden Persuaders*. New York.

13*

PRESBREY, F. (1929), *The History and Development of Advertising*. New York.

QUIRK, R. (1962), *The Use of English*. London.

ROBINS, R. H. (1964), *General Linguistics: an Introductory Survey*. London.

SAMPSON, H. (1874), *A History of Advertising from the Earliest Times*. London.

SEBEOK, T. A. (1960), ed., *Style in Language*. Cambridge, Mass.

STRANG, Barbara M. H. (1962), *Modern English Structure*. London.

STRAUMANN, H. (1935), *Newspaper Headlines*. London.

SVARTVIK, J. (1966), *On Voice in the English Verb*. The Hague.

TAYLOR, W. L. (1953), '"Cloze Procedure": A New Tool for Measuring Readability', *Journalism Quarterly*, 30, pp. 415–33.

TURNER, E. S. (1965), *The Shocking History of Advertising*. Paperback edition: Penguin Books.

ULLMANN, S. (1962), *Semantics: an Introduction to the Science of Meaning*. London.

WARBURG, J. F. (1962), *The Best-Chosen English* (*Communication Research Centre Research Papers* 1). London.

WEINREICH, U. (1963), 'On the Semantic Structure of Language', in *The Universals of Language*, ed. J. H. Greenberg, Cambridge, Mass., pp. 114–71.

WEIR, W. (1960), *On the Writing of Advertising*. New York.

WILLIAMS, R. (1962), *Britain in the Sixties: Communications*. Penguin Books.

YNGVE, V. H. (1961), 'The Depth Hypothesis', in *The Structure of Language and its Mathematical Aspects*, ed. R. Jakobson, Providence, R.I., pp. 130–8.

Index

A **boldface** number reference indicates a place where the meaning of the term is explained or discussed. Entries in SMALL CAPITALS refer to cited words or phrases.

Meaning, associative and denotative, 150, 160
—, evaluative, 129–30, 152–3, 160, 168
—, literal and figurative, 181–3
—, multiple, 175, 184
Media, 32, 58–63, 69, 85
Memorability, 27, 28–9, 189
Memory, linguistic, 29, 86–7, 176
Metaphor, 182–3
Metonymy, 183
Metre, 29, 186, 188–9, 191, 192
Modes (of discourse), 69, 85–97. See Spoken and written language, Scripted speech, Disjunctive language, Abbreviated language
Modifiers, Modification, 128–34, 169. See Pre-modifiers, Post-modifiers, Sub-modifiers, etc.
Monologue, 34, 35, 45–50, 52, 53, 54
Mood, 16, 110
Morphemes, 10, 84
Morphology, 10, 141, 154
Multiple meaning, 175, 184

NEED, 154, 155
Negatives, 30–1, 76, 77, 108, 111, 158, 159
Neologism, 141, 178, 197, 200
NEVER, 159
NEW, 52, 58, 108, 152, 153
NICE, 52, 71, 153
NO, -BODY, -ONE, etc., 159
NOT, 159
Nouns, 13, 14, 58, 128, 140
—, concrete, 58
—, abstract, 65, 167
—, proper, 132

Nouns, animate, 133
—, of time, 133
—, of place, 133
—, as modifiers, 14, 133
—, compound, 139.
    See Groups, nominal, noun
Novelty, 30, 108
NOW, 41, 124, 156
Nucleus, 21, 48, 88–9

OH-SO, 199
ONLY, 158
Operational and pragmatic skills, 5–6
Orthography, 8, 9, 21, 135, 177

Paradox, 179
Parallelism, 29, 146–7, 175, 179, 186, 190–2, 196, 197, 198
Parataxis, 18, 45, 108, 143–4, 146–7, 149
Participants, 32
—, first person, 32, 33, 35, 69, 80, 81, 82
—, second person, 32, 33, 35, 69, 80, 81, 82
—, third person, 32, 33, 180–1
—, secondary, 34, 36, 38, 45, 46, 47, 55, 82, 180–1
—, relation between, 69
Particularity of reference, 156–8
Passive voice, 81, 82, 121
Past tense, 121, 122–3
PERFECT, 58, 108
Perfective. See Aspect
Performance, Performer, 74, 85
PERHAPS, 105
Personification, 183, 184
Persuasion. See 'Loaded language'
Phonology, 8, 9, 21, 187–9